The Gospel of Faith and Justice

The Gospel of Faith and Justice

Antonio González

TRANSLATED BY JOSEPH OWENS

ORBIS BOOKS

Maryknoll, New York 10545

Founded in 1970, Orbis Books endeavors to publish works that enlighten the mind, nourish the spirit, and challenge the conscience. The publishing arm of the Maryknoll Fathers and Brothers, Orbis seeks to explore the global dimensions of the Christian faith and mission, to invite dialogue with diverse cultures and religious traditions, and to serve the cause of reconciliation and peace. The books published reflect the views of their authors and do not represent the official position of the Maryknoll Society. To learn more about Maryknoll and Orbis Books, please visit our website at www.maryknoll.org.

Library of Congress Cataloging-in-Publication Data

González, Antonio.
 [Essays. English. Selections]
 The Gospel of faith and justice / Antonio González ; translated by Joseph Owens.
  p. cm.
 Includes bibliographical references (p.   ).
 ISBN-13: 978-1-57075-611-5 (pbk.)
 1. Liberation theology. 2. Christianity and justice. I. Title.
BT83.57.G65813 2005
230'.0464—dc22
                                                                    2005011598

Contents

Introduction

The contents of these pages represent what I consider to be the best fruits of the theological project in which I have been engaged in the last few years. A guiding principle of this project has been the desire to give a radically evangelical basis to the arguments set forth by the first generation of liberation theologians. This task of radicali-zation has been much influenced by the thought and person of Ignacio Ellacuría, one of the Jesuits murdered in El Salvador in 1989.

Ellacuría had inherited from Karl Rahner the goal of providing a theological explanation of the relationship between general human history and the history of salvation. For Rahner it was still a matter of two distinct, even if "co-extensive," histories. Ellacuría went a step further, arguing that salvation concerns the one and only history of humanity, the very same history for which God has willed salvation. There can be no more than one single history, in which salvation and damnation are at stake. Ellacuría could take this step because he employed an anthropology based on the philosophy of Xavier Zubiri. Whereas Rahner's philosophy was highly influenced by Kantian themes, Zubiri's was able to overcome the dualism implicit therein and thus achieve a unitary vision.

How, then, does this salvation work itself out within the one and only history of humankind? Rahner, with his theory of the "supernatural existential," had shown that human beings, by virtue of their very existence as creatures made by God, cannot be considered as lacking in grace. Rahner concluded consequently that the idea of nature, as distinct from grace, is simply a "residual concept." Grace, as an existential, accompanies human beings from their creation. But if nature is a residual concept, then Ellacuría could go a step further and prescind from the very concept of nature in his theology of salvation: what is opposed to grace is not nature, but sin. Creation is the first salvific act of God, and the one single history of humanity is the realm wherein grace and sin are to be found in confrontation. Such reflections may appear abstract, but they have been decisive for liberation theology. Salvation occurs within the one and only history of humankind, not outside of it in some purely spiritual sphere. Even though salvation is transcendent, it directly involves our history, as is so well demonstrated in the biblical narratives. And this salvation, which is gratuitous, is in direct confrontation with sin, a real and active force in human history. This also is made clear in the biblical accounts. Through such insights a theological tradition weighed down by centuries of Constantinian and scholastic perspectives could rediscover essential aspects of the Christian message that had often been lost in dogmatic elaborations. For that reason liberation theology offered a providential opportunity for Christians of all confessions to recover the freshness of the biblical narratives and to use them as aids for interpreting the situations of poverty and oppression that plagued, and still plague, our world. It soon became clear, however, that the giant steps taken in theologies such as those of Rahner and Ellacuría were still not sufficient to respond theologically to the challenges of our time. Not all problems were definitively resolved; it was necessary to keep on thinking.

First of all it was necessary to think about the suitability of the philosophical instrument employed, and this for both theological and philosophical reasons. The weight of scholastic and neoscholastic tradition was quite perceptible in the philosophical apparatus employed by both Rahner and Ellacuría. In their philosophies, human life and praxis appeared as derivative concepts, whether derived from reflections on the evolutionary structures of the cosmos or from reflections on human subjectivity. Contemporary philosophy, however, provides us some interesting leads which, if developed properly, can lead to a philosophy of praxis understood as first philosophy. It is not a matter of a revival of Marxism, but rather of a radicalization of phenomenology, the aim being to follow through in some essential dimensions of that philosophical project and thus to overcome its traditional subjectivism. Such was the argument of my book *Estructuras de la praxis. Ensayo de una filosofía primera* (Madrid, 1997) [*Structures of Human Praxis. An Essay on First Philosophy*].

From a theological perspective, it was necessary to think carefully about what precisely constituted the efficacy of grace in human history. According to Ellacuría, human history consists of praxis. But how then does praxis relate to faith and to grace? Certainly, if praxis is understood as external works aimed at gaining one's own salvation, then praxis and grace are opposed. Liberation theology frequently seemed to be arguing for justification by one's own works. However, if praxis is the most intimate dimension of the human being, the space where our primary connection to the world is made, then grace must be found within that praxis, rendering it a gratuitous, authentic and free praxis. Whereas justification by one's own works is at root a condemnation of poor people, justification by faith could now be interpreted as a justification of the people who throughout history have been poor, rejected and condemned. To account for these possibilities, it was necessary to formulate a new theory of redemption, or atonement, which was the main intent of my volume *Teología de la praxis evangélica* (Santander, 1999) [*Theology of Evangelical Praxis*].

There still remained, however, some decisive questions to be resolved. The failure of the political projects of revolutionary transformation in Latin America and the political processes unleashed by the new phase of globalized capitalism urgently demanded theological reflection about the possibilities of new forms of social involvement for Christians. What had in fact failed were Constantinian conceptions of social change, focused on attaining political power in the national states and increasing the influence of religious leaders on political leaders. However, the biblical narratives show us another form of social change, one focused on radical transformation of the fundamental structures of the old society from their very base. Instead of gaining power, the essential strategy is renouncing power and violence; instead of the long wait for just rulers to be installed in power, possibilities are opened up *right now* for radical transformative action from the grassroots.

If we analyze seriously the reality of our world today and the different ways of responding to that world, we discover important convergences between our own times and the biblical accounts. My book *Reinado de Dios e imperio* (Santander, 2003) [*Reign of God versus Empire*] addresses precisely these matters. It includes, first, an analysis of the global capitalism that today forces itself upon the whole planet. Second, it analyzes the biblical strategies for responding to injustice and oppression, giving special attention to the responses of Jesus and the first Christian communities. Third, it examines the possibility of developing a specifically Christian response to the challenges presented in our day by the global empire of capital and violence. I believe that many readers will find my argument in this regard quite interesting, for it shows the concrete ways in which the biblical conceptions of oppression and response to oppression can be relevant in today's world.

In this respect, it is important to observe some of the signs of our times. First, our epoch is characterized by the end of the Constantinian mindset. To be sure, there are people, even entire institutions, who long for the old days of the close—even if at times critical—alliance between throne and altar. However, the processes of secularization and religious diversification have been constantly undermining Constantinianism. The church is not the same as society, and therefore it is not possible to speak of "Christian continents," as was done in the first phases of liberation theology. Between the extremes of an obsolete Christendom and a new religious individualism, the only possibility that remains is a church of communities. Yet this lone option opens up fascinating possibilities for those conceptions of Christian effectiveness centered not on gaining political power, but on more profound and diverse forms of resistance.

Second, sociological study of the emerging global society demonstrates the importance of the identity factor within that society. Contesting the idea that identity is at odds with relevance, we can readily recognize today how limited is all the seeking for social relevance in political parties, in recognized trade unions or in the power structures of the established churches. Such institutions, precisely because they have adapted themselves so perfectly to their environment, are no longer able to give voice to true dissidence. In our present time it is precisely the alternative identities that question and challenge the global empire. As a result, it is especially interesting to study certain forms of the dissent being expressed in the churches that arise among the poor; in these churches the poor are active agents with a voice of their own. With all its limitations, Latin American Pentecostalism, so often despised by theologians, is a tremendously relevant case study, for it helps us understand the concrete forms that might be assumed by a church that does not paternalistically *take care* of the poor, but is actually *made up* of the poor.

Third, we must consider what concrete tactics the new, identity-driven social movements can employ in order to begin decisive transformations of the global society. Especially interesting in this regard are phenomena such as the Latin American "popular economy," which has been studied by Chilean economist Luis Razeto, among others. There is a quite remarkable convergence between these practical accomplishments arising among the poor themselves, on the one hand, and certain theoretical considerations about the possibility of a post-capitalist economic system, on the other. Concretely, David Schweickart has argued for a post-capitalist system that, far from becoming a centrally planned state economy, is characterized by a free market vibrant with the activity of worker-managed enterprises, similar in style to those of the "popular economy." Obviously such new social structures cannot be achieved overnight, but it is clear that alternative forms of economic organization can of themselves constitute the beginnings of a new society. In this respect, the democratization of modern businesses takes on a theological significance comparable to the conversion of the households of antiquity into Christian churches.

A fourth sign of our times, one that suggests concrete forms of social and political action for Christian communities, is the growing consciousness of the relevance of non-violence. Assuredly, Christians do not opt for non-violence because of its practical effectiveness, but because of the ability of gospel non-violence to transform a human praxis ruled by the logic of retribution. All the same, we should still consider in what sense the non-violent struggle can in practice *be* effective. We do not argue that the non-violent are necessarily going to achieve greater successes than the violent. Such a thesis would be hard to prove empirically, either positively or negatively, and in any case success is not the decisive criterion for the Christian. Rather, what is essential is to observe that the effectiveness of violence is essentially limited by the means it uses. The most serious problem is not that the violent might fail. The greater problem results when the violent *triumph*, because that means they have been capable of exercising a violent power similar to that of the oppressors. And such use of violent power necessarily makes the newly powerful very similar to the formerly powerful. Those who oppose injustice by non-violent means, in contrast, are not required to resemble the oppressors; they are not even required to hold a post when the oppressors are defeated. Thus becomes visible the profound coherence between non-violence and Jesus' radical project of transforming society from its basic structures, not from a position of power.

All of this implies new strategies for social action among Christians and new possibilities for cooperation between Christians and other movements currently struggling to transform global structures of domination. I have treated these topics more extensively in the above-mentioned book, *Reinado de Dios e imperio*. The essays that follow may be considered an introduction to the theological nucleus of that text; they set forth the central reasons why we as Christians are able to offer our world a true hope of social transformation. Nonetheless, certain theological questions remain to be resolved. Both the new focus on redemption or atonement, expounded in *Teología de la praxis evangélica,* and our analysis of the social relevance of Jesus' message that appears in *Reinado de Dios e imperio*, point necessarily towards a Christology. The so-called "third quest" for the historical Jesus offers new possibilities for Christology that need to be raised to a systematic reflection. Some of the keys for such reflection are offered in the reflections that follow.

In any case, these reflections have no other aim than helping the reader to encounter the radical novelty of the God of the gospels. That God, not our poor theologies, is the one who has made his own the cause of the poor and is the one who will finally be shown to be the Lord of history.

I would like especially to thank Joseph Owens for his interest and dedicated labor, which have made this book possible.

1

The Continuing Vitality
of Liberation Theology

Nowadays it is commonly accepted that the term "liberation theology" designates not so much a determined system of thought, endowed with specified contents and an internal structure, but rather a theological movement, one that sometimes includes the pastoral practice from which it arises and which it accompanies. Liberation theology cannot be simply identified with "Latin American theology," not only because there have arisen African and Asian theologies that also understand themselves to be liberation theologies, but also because not all Latin American theology has gladly accepted the label. Such reluctance is not necessarily due to the desires for originality which each theologian might have, but rather is due to the objective diversity of theological undertakings. Without entering into intramural arguments, we will here refer to liberation theology as a theological movement with worldwide dimensions and a plural structure.

For that reason, it would be too bold for us to speak of "the" method of "the" theology of liberation. In the case of a theological movement that is plural and widely diffused, it is difficult to think in terms of unicity of method. Rather than speak of "method," we could possibly speak of some basic ideas which, without marking boundaries of inclusion and exclusion, make up the core of a set of intuitions that inspires the work of diverse theologians in different parts of the world who attempt to respond to a diversity of problems. Gustavo Gutiérrez was probably the first to formulate these intuitions when he stated that liberation theology is grounded in two key discoveries: the primacy of practice and the perspective of the poor. In this article I would like to argue that the relevance of these two principles is vital for all future theology, regardless of whether or not it is called liberation theology.

THE PRIMACY OF PRACTICE

At times the phrase "primacy of practice" has been understood as unequivocal proof that perverse Marxist influences had infected liberation theology. Certainly, Marx was one of the pioneers, after Hegel, in demonstrating the philosophical relevance of praxis as an alternative to idealism. Even St. Basil in his time, however, taught that action is the beginning of knowledge, and more recently Maurice Blondel has made action the starting point for Catholic apologetics. Contemporary philosophy, in both its analytic and its phenomenological currents, has paid increasingly more attention to action. The North American pragmatists, some Latin American philosophies and the German transcendental pragmatists are also worth mentioning in this regard. Of course, mentioning certain thinkers and tendencies is not enough to justify a particular theological position. Rather, the relevance of this fundamental intuition of liberation theology needs to be grounded philosophically and theologically.

Naturally, we do not pretend to accomplish that task here, but we do wish to stress its importance. Christian theology does not have now at its disposal, as it did in former times, a system of commonly accepted philosophical truths. To the contrary, the crisis of the Aristotelian-Thomistic scholastic system has opened the way for an eclectic utilization of very diverse philosophical positions. This development has decidedly enriched the treatment of many theological topics—one need only think of the importance of the discovery of the essential historicity of human being for our present understanding of revelation. The downside of this diversity of philosophical resources is the frequent deference of theologians to different philosophical fashions. Thus, for example, when European intellectual trends dictate dialectical negatives, the Eucharist is a dialectical negative. When they dictate communities of dialogue, then the Eucharist becomes a communicative unity. No doubt there is some value in adapting to these fashions, but the result can be a dilettantism that not only fails to penetrate into real problems, but also produces the impression that in theology one can say anything, provided it sounds good to the listeners, be they conservative or progressive.

It is important therefore that theology be concerned with a rigorous justification of the philosophy it uses. If liberation theology understands its starting point to be located in praxis, it cannot simply have recourse to any philosophy that in some fashion coincides with that interest. It is necessary to show philosophically that such a starting point is truly justified. This may not be a task which is proper to the theologian, but it is a task which is urgently necessary for theology. In a world where human bonds become increasingly tighter, we are ever more conscious not only of the planet's cultural diversity, but also of the great social, economic and ecological problems that affect the whole of humanity. The starting point of theology determines in a crucial way the perspective that will be used to approach these problems theologically. If theology were to base itself, for example, on the question about the *meaning* of life, then cultural dialogue among different cosmovisions would occupy the foreground of interest, while other human problems would be relegated to the background or would be excluded from the field of theology. The appropriate choice of a starting point for theology can influence significantly the formulation of the message that Christianity desires to communicate to a humanity besieged by enormous conflicts.

In ancient times Christianity believed that its preaching concerned all aspects of human reality, understood then as nature. Nowadays we are confronted with an enormous diminution of those original pretensions. Those who accuse liberation theology of being reductionist have often done so because of a previous, radical reduction of Christianity to a mere cosmovision that gives meaning to life and has ethical implications. Theology must strive to overcome this one-sidedness, which threatens to convert Christianity into a jumble of empty words and tedious moral duties. The reign of God, according to St. Paul, does not consist in words but in a dynamism (1 Cor 4:20). Certainly we can no longer think of the human person as "nature," for such a conception would leave out essential aspects, such as the operative presence of grace and our real (not just conceived) historicity. *Activity*, on the other hand, can be a way of theological access both to the human person, considered integrally, and to the action of grace. Christianity is a dynamism aroused by Christ in history, not simply a religious and moral cosmovision of the world.

The primacy of practice as a starting point for theology is naturally charged with ecumenical relevance. The church conflicts which occurred during the Protestant Reformation have as a backdrop, along with many other historical factors, the confrontation between naturalism and subjectivism as conceptions of the human person and the work of grace in the person. If theology has its starting point in *action*, it might possibly discover there a way of overcoming the conflict between faith and works, by showing that both faith and law constitute dimensions inscribed within human action. This insight could also be important for the dialogue between Christianity and other religions. From the times of Spanish neoscholasticism up to contemporary theologies of religion it has been repeatedly stated that the different religions find their meeting point in the practice of justice. Such affirmations have often tended towards a certain moralism, from which liberation theology is not exempt. Such moralism is not only a type of reductionism, but a serious distortion of the religious experience, especially of the Christian religious experience. This problem would be avoided if it were shown that the practice of justice is not simply the moral consequence of a religious cosmovision, but a privileged sphere for finding grace and faith, even in non-Christian religions.

To this end we need serious theological and philosophical reflection. The primacy of practice cannot mean simply the tyranny of pastoral immediacies. The huge pastoral problems that Christianity must confront in the near future require rigorous theoretical work, without which we will never be able to respond satisfactorily to many challenges that are new and unexpected. We must wonder whether the great renewal movement which arose in the Catholic church out of the Second Vatican Council has not been partially truncated due to lack of concern for adequate intellectual formation. We behold complete religious congregations, once characterized by high levels of philosophical and theological learning, committing themselves with frenzied generosity to the most immediate apostolic tasks, but neglecting all systematic reflection based on their praxis. The most urgent or most obvious tasks are not necessarily the most important or the most practical ones. We should not be surprised if many Christians, when they can find no serious theological reflection about their pressing problems, return to the secure formulas of yesteryear. Perhaps the present intellectual winter of the Catholic church is not only a consequence of the so-called "involution," but also an important cause of the same.

THE PERSPECTIVE OF THE POOR

The "perspective of the poor" is the other great intuition that shapes the method of liberation theology. If the primacy of practice is susceptible to philosophical grounding, the perspective of the poor appears to constitute a strictly theological criterion. We are dealing here with probably one of the greatest graces that the Spirit has granted to the churches in the second half of the twentieth century. Certainly, poverty as the realm for encountering God constitutes an essential theme of Christian spirituality of all epochs. Despite the great failures of the church in this regard, it has never quite forgotten this essential dimension of the gospel of Jesus Christ. However, the Christian conscience has not always had the same intense realization of how poverty takes on concrete human faces in the truly impoverished of our world. When such concrete poverty becomes, in all its dimensions, a theological locus of the first magnitude, then we find ourselves without a doubt before something radically new in the history of Christian theology.

The justification of this starting point requires rigorous theological reflection. Certainly, the perspective of the poor as a privileged place for our encounter with the merciful and faithful God of Christian revelation is by no means a legacy of theologians, who rather reflect at a level removed from the experience of many Christians. Theologians are still obliged, however, to concern themselves with understanding this experience by employing the exegetical, historical and conceptual resources which are proper to theological work. Liberation theology doubtless passed through an initial phase in which its great intuitions were discovered and formulated, but now its effectiveness as a theological movement must be demonstrated in its ability to ground and to systematize those discoveries. In European libraries, liberation theology texts usually appear in the pastoral theology section. Such prejudice perhaps reveals a certain petulance on the part of the old theology, but it may be seen as having some foundation if liberation theology does not progress beyond its initial intuitions and programs.

Such systematic elaboration of the major contents of theology would also serve to show that liberation theology does not consist in simple reflection on the moral consequences of the Christian message. Indeed, the perspective of the poor as theology's starting point would be tainted if it were to lose its eminently gratuitous character. Occasionally, certain theologians have given reason for our interpreting their discourse as primarily moral, and no doubt the Christian message has a constitutive moral dimension. However, the irruption of the poor, both into the life of the churches and into theological reflection, is above all a grace from God. This grace has led to a profound renewal of Christian spirituality, religious life and pastoral ministry. The radicality of this grace may also be seen in the way that it enables theology to interpret the contents of the Christian faith beneath the light with which the poor have illuminated the church.

Theology must naturally think also about the ethical consequences of Christian faith. In this regard liberation theology, as much as it may wish to treat many other traditional moral topics which need to be updated, will certainly have to continue to show special interest in the problems of social ethics. The changes which have taken place in the world order need to be rigorously pondered and deliberated. To this end theology will require independence from those who cynically climb onto the bandwagon of the victors, as if temporal triumphs represented some kind of theological confirmation (hardly in keeping with what happened to Jesus!). Theology must also steer clear of the dogmatism of those who can think only by making use of old formulas. Theology's need to seek alternatives to the reigning world disorder derives not from fidelity to any doctrine or any utopia, but from the emaciated faces of the earth's defeated. It is precisely these faces that call for social thought which can confront honestly and radically the grave problems which humanity suffers. In many cases the situation of the poor has gotten worse since the end of the cold war, and it is the poor who continue to make liberation theology a matter of urgency.

Both in systematic theology and in social ethics the perspective of the poor has induced a restless mood, not only for doing theology, but for having a Christian view of the world. The Augustinian restlessness of the human heart continues to be an essential character of Christian life regarding this world. Conservative thought would like to convince itself and to convince others that the world is fine the way it is, or at least that it cannot be better. As a result, when conservatives do theology, they tend to place themselves in a position we might call "Hegelian." The theologian installs himself in the mind of God and from that vantage point attempts to clarify for us what is happening in the world. Evil, pain, suffering and poverty are then "explained" and thereby justified theologically. Of course, this way of thinking ends up in contradiction to the cross of Christ (cf. Phil 3:18), which comes to be excluded from such theology. Liberation theology can never fail to insist upon the mysterious character of a God who, instead of justifying the world's suffering, personally takes it upon himself. The perspective of the poor is irreconcilable with the perspective of the absolute spirit. We should never attempt to convert theology into a tribunal for judging God and creatures.

Unfortunately, theology, especially in the Catholic church, knows a lot about tribunals. The problems of ecclesial misunderstanding which have beset liberation theology have not generally concerned the integrity of its dogma. In fact, first world theologies, to which church censors frequently have recourse, represent in many cases greater challenges to Catholic tradition; we need consider only the fideism or the rationalism of many of the theologies currently in use. The difficulties which liberation theology has faced are due fundamentally to its questioning of church structure. The Catholic church is governed, in fact and in great measure, by the secure bureaucracy of the Vatican state, a bureaucracy which lacks all basis in scripture or tradition and which exercises its power through a corps of career diplomats who by profession are closer to the centers of political and economic power than they are to the real poverty of the majority of Catholics. The collegiality of the bishops around the successor of Peter has little to do with this structure. As long as the structural submission of the church of Christ to this spurious system of government is not corrected, it will be difficult to expect the church to adopt authentically, not just rhetorically, the perspective of the poor.

The challenge of the poor majority also confronts liberation theology itself. The theologian, like any intellectual, is not immune to the temptations proper to his office, such as vanity, acommodation or desire for facile praise. These temptations are capable of ruining any intellectual vocation by driving it towards unproductive superficiality. In the case of the theologian the risks are greater, since the seeking out of receptive audiences in the first world can end up obscuring the very thing that theology wants to help to proclaim: the gospel of Jesus Christ. All the more is this the case in a theology which proposes to take on explicitly the perspective of the poor. The mass media of consumer society frequently find themselves in conflict with a church that opposes the patterns of conduct that they are trying to promote. It is unfortunate that this confrontation is often due less to the prophetic charism of first world Christians than to their conservatism. However that may be, liberation theology ought to possess sufficient astuteness so as not to be converted into a type of formulaic church liberalism that is closer to presumably progressive sectors of the first world than it is to the poor majority of the third.

To avoid these pitfalls nothing is more effective than real proximity to the poor, accompanied by a profound commitment to the intellectual task which the church so needs. When the poor approach the church, they do not do so primarily in search of financing from a European NGO for their chickens, nor do they hope to hear great moralizing harangues. Rather they seek to utter and to listen to an authentic word of faith. The growth of Pentecostal groups among the most impoverished sectors of society cannot be explained solely by sociological factors or solely attributed to the shady machinations of the United States. In the Catholic church, probably due to the way its clergy are trained, there is a certain inability, on both the right and the left, to proclaim the faith without falling into several traps: repetition of dogmatic formulas, presumedly secularizing explanations of the same dogmas or heavily moralizing sermons. Years ago one could presuppose the existence of great masses of people anchored in Catholic popular religiosity. Today this is no longer the reality of the poor of Asia or of Africa, and probably not of great parts of

Latin America either. What the poor desperately need seems not to be either a secular critique of their traditional religiosity or a demonstration of its moral consequences. Rather, theology must help to articulate a language of faith which originates *with* the poor and forges liberating connections with their situation. That task requires both nearness to their situation and rigorous intellectual work.

BY WAY OF CONCLUSION

The basic intuitions which characterize the liberation theology movement continue to be the source of great theoretical and practical challenges, not only for the powerful of this world and for certain ecclesiastical sectors linked with them, but also for liberation theology itself. Responding to these challanges requires renewed fidelity to the Spirit of Jesus and serious intellectual work. Eschewing vain intellectual fashions and undue fidelity to formulas or ideologies, liberation theology continues to exemplify the will to develop a body of thought which responds faithfully to the needs of the poor of this planet. It may be that the poor have already been abandoned by the ideologies and the fashions of the first world. Possibly for that reason liberation theology is no longer fashionable there. Actually, that would be a good sign. If liberation theology is not in fashion and theology still continues to be done according to its basic intuitions, then liberation theology was in the end not just a fashion. Theologians are not singers or athletes who have to appear continually in the mass media (or before the tribunals of the Inquisition) in order to maintain their self-esteem. Perhaps rigorous work pursued in obscurity is the best way to be faithful to those who live and die in obscurity.

Indeed, the theological project of liberation theology appears to be particularly suited to do the kind of theology that our times require. Sri Lankan theologian Tissa Balasuriya has already spoken from Asia about the need for a "planetary theology." Indeed, the basic contents of the Christian faith need to be reconceived within a horizon which is no longer the Greek horizon of nature or the European horizon of subjectivity. No Christian theology can ignore the plain fact that the majority of humankind (and the majority of Catholics as well) is impoverished. Even while defending the unquestionable richness of theological pluralism, we believe there are good reasons for claiming that the basic intuitions of liberation theology not only have continuing validity, but can also be fundamental ingredients for any theology seeking to do the planetary-level reflection that the new century requires.

2

The Gospel of Faith and Justice

Often one hears many Christians in the so-called third world stating that the times of the Exodus are now past and that we find ourselves in a time which is more like that of Job or of Ecclesiastes.[1] What they mean is that the hopes for rapid social changes, aimed at improving the situation of millions of impoverished poor people, have faded into the distance. It is as if there were no hopes within our reach, but still we must go on denouncing the continuing suffering of innocents like Job, and still we must maintain, like Qoheleth, a critical watch upon the world, even though that critical watch can achieve little to bring about a social transformation that will do away with injustice in the near future.

By no means do I wish to negate the importance that the books of Job or Ecclesiastes still have today for the Christian. Nonetheless, forgetting the perspective of Exodus can be a grave error for those Christians who are conscious that their faith is in some way connected to the problem of social justice in the world. It is not just that the Book of Exodus is perennially relevant for getting to the heart of Christian faith and its contribution to social justice. The problem, rather, is that the perspective mentioned above accepts too readily the despairing idea that the alternatives to the massive injustice of our world are situated in a distant future.

"Hope," Archbishop Romero used to say, "will soon be a reality." The failures of certain political groups, certain economic systems or certain public figures in no way cancel out, from a biblical perspective, the nearness of this reality. Nor is it a question of changing Christian hope into an otherworldly promise, an existential attitude or a consoling sentiment. Hope for an effective and real overcoming of social injustice is not, from a biblical viewpoint, a hope for the future. It is a hope for today, realizable in the present moment in which these lines are being written or read.

The tendency to situate hope in a distant future and to take refuge in a more or less despairing criticism of the present not only introduces too many "roots of bitterness" (Heb 12:15) into the Christian community, but also quite likely reflects an inadequate understanding of the biblical message about faith and justice. No one advances without learning from one's errors, and no one learns from one's errors without admitting to making them. In order for Christians today to advance in the way of faith and justice, they must learn from the errors of the past. And for that there is nothing better than to ask ourselves anew, with the candor of one who can still learn (Mt 18:3), what it is that Christian faith says about and brings to the problem of social justice.

"ABRAHAM BELIEVED AND IT WAS RECKONED TO HIM AS JUSTICE"

At times the relationship between Christian faith and social justice has been expressed in a purely extrinsic and moralist manner. The Christian, by reason of being so, must behave ethically, and this ethical behavior must include commitment to all the just causes of humanity. When it is discovered that this does no more than articulate the universal obligations of all human beings, without clarifying what is specific to faith, an attempt is made to convert the historical Jesus into an eminent model of dedication to the universal struggle for justice, again without it becoming clear what specifically is the Christian contribution to that struggle.

In reality, the link between faith and justice is much more intrinsic and radical than any universal ethical obligation. The scriptures, in addition to recognizing universal ethical obligations, also question the ability of any moralism, even a politically correct moralism, to effectively change the world. From the biblical viewpoint, the relationship between faith and justice constitutes a gospel, a piece of good news, which irrupts into a world of oppression and opens up a way of justice which that world by itself could barely imagine. Christian faith not only affirms that a way towards justice already exists, but affirms as well that this new way, though impossible for human beings, no matter how moral they are, is nevertheless possible for God (Mk 10:27).

The good news of the intrinsic relationship between faith and justice becomes visible in the first pages of the scriptures, when we read the story of how Abraham "believed YHWH, who reckoned it to him as justice" (Gen 15:6). If we read this text from a structural perspective, situating it in the canonical context, it becomes clear that we are not dealing here with an event which has to do only with Abraham as an individual, and which can therefore be reduced to existentialist or psychological interpretations. We behold an event which, from a biblical viewpoint, is decisive for all the history of humanity and for God's plan for that humanity.

In the course of nine chapters (Gen 3-11), the book of Genesis presents us with a dismal panorama of human history. The text does not seek to be simply historical or etiological, but rather to speak about the present. For that reason the history, which begins with the sin of Adam, ends in the present time of the possible editors of the text: with the tower of Babel, symbol of the great oppressor empires like Babylon. The text has even fewer historiographic pretensions if we include the story of Adam, in which the protagonist himself bears a name that represents all of us: he is called precisely *adam*, that is, "human being." The history of Adam is the history of every human being, and that history is realized and shaped amidst the structures of oppression, incarnated in the text through the great empires of antiquity. If we replace the tower of Babel with the massive skyscrapers that serve as physical displays of the supremacy of the worldwide capitalist system, and if we replace Adam with each and every one of us, we will draw quite close to what the text wants to communicate to us, and therefore also to what the history of Abraham means for our time.

The heart of the text's message is that Abraham, in contrast to Adam, believed in God's promise. Adam preferred to believe the word of the serpent, who promises human beings that they will be like gods, eating the fruits, good and bad, of their own actions (Gen 3:5). Just as God the Creator makes all things good (Gen 1:31), the human being ("Adam") would be like God, making himself good by means of the fruit of his own actions. However, the person who wishes to justify himself through the fruit of his

own actions not only does not become like God, but makes himself a slave of those creatures ("serpents") who, by putting themselves in God's place, seek to guarantee for us a correspondence
between our praxis and its results. The outcomes are idolatry and
generalized injustice, two sides of the same coin according to biblical thought:

1) Whoever wishes to justify himself by the fruit of his own
actions must come to view God as an enemy, whose judgment
about his praxis ought to be feared (Gen 3:8-10). Once embarked
on this logic, human beings can do no less than offer to the divinity the results of their own work, even though God has never asked
them for such sacrifices. It is difficult to find a more severe critique of the origins of institutionalized religion (Gen 4:1-5). The
alternative to religious slavery can be some renewed attempt to
become divine by uniting oneself to the divinity and producing
"supermen," even though such attempts are ridiculous not only to
the Creator God, but also to the simple forces of nature (Gen 6-9).

2) Whoever wishes to justify himself by the fruit of his own
actions must necessarily use other people to produce this fruit,
thus falling into a game of mutual manipulations and accusations
which can only provoke mistrust and the oppression of some human beings by others (Gen 3:7,11-16). The desire for self-justification can only lead to envy and murder, for the fruit of others'
actions places one's own achievements in question. And the attempt to make the murderers receive the merited consequences of
their actions introduces an unstoppable logic of vengeance (Gen
4:23). The state, symbolized by the tower of Babel, can attempt to
monopolize violence, but the price is institutionalized domination
of some over others. Without a doubt, whoever wishes to justify
himself seeks power in order to produce results, and desires other
people's admiration of the fruit obtained; that means, however,
that other people can be, for the powerful, only subjects or admirers. States, with their intrinsic tendency to divinize themselves, do
not unite, but rather divide, humanity into diverse national and
linguistic factions (Gen 11).

3) Whoever wishes to justify himself by the fruit of his own
actions draws everyone around him into the mad race to produce
results, a race that can only bring about human alienation in work
and the destruction of the entire planet. Paradoxically, the final

result obtained in this mad race of self-justification is only death (Gen 3:17-19).

After this depressing description of the various aspects of human injustice in relation to God, to others and to the earth itself, the scriptures present us with the election of Abraham. In fact, each of the human sins narrated before that election was accompanied by a word of grace and mercy on God's part (Gen 3:21; 4:15; 9:15). After the narrative about the tower of Babel no specific word of grace appears, because the word of grace is none other than the election of Abraham and, with it, the beginning of salvation history, presented in the rest of the Bible.

For a mentality influenced by a certain philosophizing universalism, the particularity of Abraham's election causes certain problems. Some might wish that God establish moral principles or religious norms that all people could discover by themselves in all cultures, and God's salvific action would be reduced to that. The particularity of divine election and the particularity of the chosen nomad pastor are a scandal for many. Nonetheless, biblical thought on this point is completely unanimous and coherent: human beings cannot return to paradise on their own (Gen 3:23-24), precisely because that return to paradise would be a result of their own actions and would not rescue them from the infernal and serpentine logic in which their pretension to self-justification envelops them. It is precisely the particularity of election that shows that the definitive overcoming of injustice is not, like the tower of Babel, a human work, but an initiative of God.

Still, an accurate account of the meaning of Abraham's election is not to be found in predestinationism or in Pelagianism. What is at stake in this election is not the problem of individual salvation, but the problem of the divine answer to a world dominated by injustice, oppression and lust for power. For that very reason, the particularity of the election does not lose sight of the universal perspective: "by you," says YHWH to Abraham, "all the families of the earth shall bless themselves" (Gen 12:3). The very name that God gives him, "Abraham," alludes to this universal dimension of his election (Gen 17:5). In biblical thought, the particularity of the election is at the service of a plan which concerns the whole human race. For that reason the history of the patriarchs is inserted into the wider history of all humanity, within which it acquires its meaning. Paul will push this idea to an extreme when he states that even the failure of the election fulfills a function for the benefit of all humanity (Rom 9-11).

The particularity of the election means, at the very start, a rupture with a humanity under the rule of injustice: "Go from your country and your kindred and your father's house to the land that I will show you" (Gen 12:1). So Abraham leaves Haran, the center of the lunar cult, and sets out for the unknown. Any solution to the problem of injustice which seeks and obtains the approval of the majority has something suspicious about it (Lk 6:26). But this call to break away does not lead Abraham to solitude or individualism. On the contrary, Abraham's calling includes the promise of a people and a land: "I will make of you a great nation, and I will bless you" (Gen 12:2). Thus follows the great importance of the offspring: "Look toward heaven, and number the stars, if you are able to number them . . . So shall your descendents be" (Gen 15:5).

With this we touch the nucleus of the biblical conception of salvation. God's alternative to injustice comes through the formation of a different people, chosen from among the peoples of the earth. In order to form this people, it is not primarily great moral or political works that are asked of Abraham, but above all faith in the God who calls him. If injustice, from the biblical viewpoint, has its deepest root in "Adam's" lack of faith, the history of justice begins at the point where someone believes God, and not the serpent. Abraham believed and it was reckoned to him as justice (Gen 15:6). Obviously it is not a purely individual or interior faith, alien to human praxis: it is rather a faith which puts Abraham on the road with all his family. It is precisely this faith that makes possible a new praxis in history: faced with the idea, proper to Semitic peoples, that God requires the sacrifice of the firstborn son, Abraham does not sacrifice Isaac. Faith not only gives Abraham the willingness to lose what he most loves, but also allows a rupture with the religious conventions around him. Without faith the rupture is not possible, and without the rupture there is no newness in history. Not without reason will Paul say that true descent from Abraham, that which makes us members of the chosen people, is not biological, but comes through faith (Gal 3:7).

Clearly the injustice originating today within the imperial systems of power and prestige has its ultimate root in the lack of faith of the human being ("Adam") who insists on attaining his own justification. In the face of such faithlessness, the new justice which God introduces into history starts from the faith of a tiny group of nomads, situated on the margins of the great states of the time. These two elements—imperial power and the people of Abraham—constitute precisely the two protagonists who confront one another in the account of Exodus. The Egyptian empire has enslaved the descendents of Abraham. Out of this confrontation arises the biblical model for liberation from injustice.

"OUR JUSTICE WILL BE TO PUT THESE COMMANDMENTS INTO PRACTICE"

The Exodus is the center of Israel's faith. No other sapiential text, important as it may be, can replace what constitutes the confession of faith for an Israelite:

> A wandering Aramean was my father; and he went down into Egypt and sojourned there, few in number; and there he became a nation, great, mighty, and populous. And the Egyptians treated us harshly, and afflicted us, and laid upon us hard bondage. Then we cried out to YHWH, the God of our fathers, and YHWH heard our voice, and saw our affliction, our toil, and our oppression; and YHWH brought us out of Egypt with a mighty hand and an outstretched arm, with great terror, with signs and wonders; and he brought us into this place and gave us this land, a land flowing with milk and honey. (Deut 26:5-9)

What is most notable in these accounts is the clear linkage that the faith of Israel establishes between misery and human responsibility. Poverty is not presented as a result of fate, divine design or poor people's own actions. Poverty is associated directly with the oppression of some human beings by others. The Egyptians brutally enslave the Israelites (Ex 1:8-14). These accounts are perfectly coherent with those of Genesis. This is well worth remembering in these times when both "conservatives" and "progressives" tend to be complacent about the powers and the rules that prevail in our world. In any case, what clearly does not fit in with the usual "conservative" or "progressive" conceptions is the alternative to oppression that the Exodus story proposes as the alternative desired by God. Let us examine it more closely.

It is noteworthy that the book of Exodus, before introducing us to YHWH's alternative to oppression, presents us first with several more obvious and more usual alternatives, even while showing us the relative inefficacy of all of them.

1) In the first place, we have the "passive resistance" of the Israelite midwives, who delay in carrying out Pharaoh's order to eliminate the newborn males. This is a very frequent path of resistance among peoples who have been oppressed for ages ("of course, boss, we'll take care of it right now . . ."). The midwives' strategy, however, does not change in the least the policy of Pharaoh, who hands the genocidal task over to the Egyptians themselves (Ex 1:15-22).

2) Second, what we may call "individual charity" does not seem very effective either. The daughter of Pharaoh takes pity on the Hebrew baby abandoned on the waters of the Nile. This attitude of helping "the orphan and the widow," which is consistent with the ethics of the Ancient East (not just Israel!), may be providential for the task which Moses will carry out in the future, but in itself the charity of Pharaoh's daughter does not change the situation of the Hebrews, who continue to be oppressed.

3) Third, Moses' recourse to violence against the oppressors also changes nothing. Doubtless the text is quite realistic in presenting Moses' violence as a response to the prior violence of the system: Moses kills the Egyptian who strikes a Hebrew. But the violence not only provokes the mistrust of the oppressed themselves toward their would-be liberator, but also unleashes the system's violent reaction against Moses, who has to go into exile (Ex 2:11-22). In the end, the situation of the oppressed has not changed at all, as the text tells us clearly (Ex 2:23).

4) What of a more "moderate" path, that of negotiations which seek an "agreement" with the oppressors? Moses and Aaron undertake a dialogue with Pharaoh. Seemingly, they do not ask for great changes in the system, only a slight improvement in the labor conditions of the Hebrews. Concretely, Moses and Aaron re-

quest three feast days (Ex 5:3). Nonetheless the negotiation fails, and Pharaoh makes the Hebrews' working conditions even harder. The Israelite laborers can only feel betrayed by their representatives (Ex 5:1-6:1).

5) Finally, the story of the plagues shows us an Egyptian empire on the verge of collapsing. Confronted by God, by its workers and by the natural environment, the system enters into full crisis. Pharaoh finds himself discredited, but stubbornly keeps up the oppression. Moses, by contrast, enjoys great authority among the Egyptians themselves and their leaders (Ex 11:3). One might think that the moment had arrived for Moses to take power and make the changes necessary in the system. The biblical history had already recounted the precedent of a Hebrew in the government of the empire—Joseph. As Pharaoh's chief steward, Joseph had arranged for the state to take over the means of production, thus making possible the overcoming of famine in a moment of crisis (Gen 47:13-26).

However, the central proposal of Exodus is very different. God does not seek to enthrone Moses in the palace of Pharaoh, but to create an alternative community on the periphery of the system. And that community is none other than the people of Israel settled in the promised land. It was not a question of a transformation or reform of the system, but of the creation by God of something radically new in history: an alternative community in which there would be no room for the injustices that occur in the oppressive systems that hold sway over the world. Let us examine this in more detail.

a) First, as in the case of Abraham, we are dealing with a departure, a rupture, an exodus. The biblical proposal has little interest in the idea of seizing political power in order to transform society from within Pharaoh's palace. This type of solution generally entrusts the overcoming of injustice to some type of elite or vanguard, which exercises power in the name of the oppressed, while promising that in the future all oppression will disappear. By contrast, the biblical solution begins the construction of a new society right now, and that construction is not entrusted to a new group of power-brokers, but comes from the oppressed themselves, who begin from this very moment a new form of society on the periphery of the system. It is the radicality of creating something totally new: an alternative system. Precisely because the newness is greater, so too are the rupture and the risk.

b) Second, the new society responds to an initiative of God and is not the simple result of human efforts: "YHWH your God is not giving you this good land to possess because of your righteousness" (Deut 9:6). The image of God's parting the waters of the sea so that the Israelites might pass through alludes to God the Creator, who separates the primeval waters in order to make a place for a world that is habitable (Gen 1:6-7). Indeed, the radicality of the biblical idea of creation does not come from philosophical speculations, but from the experience of God's creating something new in history: a different society in which the injustices of the empires are not repeated.

c) God's initiative establishes, then, a difference between this God and all the other gods of the other peoples. Psalm 82 presents God entering into the assembly of gods and reproaching them for being incapable of solving the problem of injustice. Biblical monotheism does not derive primarily from philosophical speculation, but from the experience that the God of Abraham and Moses is a God capable of saving his people, in contrast to all the idols created by human hands. These idols, though they promise salvation, do no more than create dependency, legitimatizing different systems of oppression. For that very reason the new society created by God makes the foundations of the earth tremble (Ps 82:5).

d) If the initiative comes from God, what is asked of the new community is above all faith in God's promises, a faith that allows them to begin a journey, abandon the oppressive system and leave behind the other inadequate solutions: "The people believed, and when they heard that YHWH had visited the people of Israel and that he had seen their affliction, they bowed their heads and worshiped" (Ex 4:31). Without the people's faith in the promises of God, the radical liberation from injustice proposed in Exodus would not have taken place.

e) The faith that makes it possible to set off on a journey is not the faith of an individual, but the faith of a concrete community. The liberation from Egypt is not possible without the existence of a community of faith, which is able to discern the congruence between the new proposals of YHWH and the old promises of the God of Abraham, Isaac and Jacob—and to recognize in both cases the actions of one and the same Lord (Ex 3:13-15). Liberation from injustice, in the biblical model, does not consist in the enunciation of grand ethical or political principles, but rather in God's history with a concrete people that believes in him, that cries to him and that hopes in him out of the depths of injustice.

f) Liberation from injustice, however, not only presupposes a community, but also creates it. It creates a community not on racial or linguistic bases, but on the initiative of God. This initiative is sufficiently attractive so as to draw into the new community a great multitude of oppressed people who are not Israelites (descendents of Israel), but who, with the Israelites, believe in the initiative of God, set out on a journey and come to form a single new people (Ex 12:37-38).

g) Only within the context of God's initiative and the existence of a believing community is it possible to understand leadership such as that of Moses. Apart from that initiative and without the existence of a believing community, there is little sense in our identifying certain persons or movements as "new Moseses," since they normally end up defrauding the oppressed people. Still, placed in an appropriate context, the figure of Moses is especially instructive, because it shows us not only how necessary it is that leadership be autochthonous, but also how necessary it is that such leadership be profoundly knowledgeable both of the culture of the oppressors and also of the culture of the oppressed. Without that double experience, it is impossible to talk about an "alternative," for every alternative presupposes a dialectic between two terms whose deep structure must be known in order not to repeat, with new formulas, the very reality that is being rejected.

h) The project of the alternative society is spelled out in an "instruction" (torah), in a "law" designed to ensure that the oppression of Egypt is not repeated (Ex 23:9). The meaning of Israel's law is comprehensible only on the basis of the prior liberation from injustice (Deut 6:20-25). Thus it contains provisions for the introduction of such institutions as the forgiveness of debts every seven years (Deut 15:1-6), the prohibition of lending with interest (Deut 23:19-20) and the recuperation of one's own lands every fifty years (Lv 25:8-12). The community of Israel was to become a land of refuge for slaves who fled from other nations (Deut 23:15-16), and the Israelite slaves were to be freed periodically (Ex 21:1-

11; Lv 25:35-55; Deut 15:12-18). Other measures were aimed at insuring an appropriate relationship with the environment, by allowing rest for the cultivated land (Lv 25:1-7). In this way the law seeks to guarantee a new form of life in which there will no longer be poor people (Deut 15:4): "It will be righteousness for us, if we are careful to do all this commandment before YHWH our God, as he has commanded us" (Deut 6:25).

i) These are not simply paternalistic measures, recommending that the powerful take care of the orphan and the widow without relinquishing their power. Such concern already existed in the neighboring cultures, even in the great oppressor empires. Hammurabi himself boasts in his famous code about caring for the orphan and the widow. The new society created by God is inspired by a fraternal and highly egalitarian ethos. For that reason the law does not necessarily foresee the existence of a king in Israel (Deut 17:14). In fact, the tribes of Israel lived for about two hundred years without a monarchy, as a "segmentarian and acephalous" society, to use the terms of anthropologists. Upon the introduction of the monarchy, the law foresees (whether *post factum* or not, it matters little) a strict division of powers between the judges, the king, the priests and the prophets (Deut 16:18-18:22). This radically differentiates Israel from the neighboring societies, in which all religious and political powers were concentrated in a single person. The power of the king himself was to be limited, not only materially (in terms of arms and money), but above all formally: the king is subject to the law, and not above it, and therefore he must carry it with him and read it every day of his life (Deut 17:16-19). Thus "his heart will not be lifted up above his brethren" (Deut 17:20), the other Israelites.

j) In this way Israel was ordained to become an alternative society, placed by God in the midst of the other peoples, and destined to attract their notice and draw them to the way of life instituted by Moses:

> Behold, I have taught you statutes and ordinances, as YHWH my God commanded me, that you should do them in the land which you are entering to take possession of it. Keep them and do them, for that will be your wisdom and your understanding in the sight of the peoples, who, when they hear all these

statutes, will say, "Surely, this great nation is a wise and understanding people." For what great nation is there that has a god so near to it as YHWH our God is to us, whenever we call upon him? And what great nation is there that has statutes and ordinances so righteous as all this law which I set before you this day? (Deut 4:5-8)

Now it becomes clear that the necessary rupture and the separation of Israel as a people that stands in contrast with all the other peoples does not mean sectarian isolationism, but an alternative. Simply by being distinct, and at the same time an attractive alternative, the people of Israel was called to be a blessing for all nations.

"ALL OUR RIGHTEOUS DEEDS ARE LIKE A POLLUTED GARMENT"

The history of Israel, as recounted and interpreted in the scriptures, obviously reveals a failure, at least partial, of the people in carrying out its mission. As the prophet Isaiah says: "We were with child, we writhed, we have as it were brought forth wind. We have wrought no deliverance in the earth, and the inhabitants of the world cannot bring it forth" (Is 26:18). Possibly many people committed to social justice in recent years have at some point felt the same way. No doubt many social justice projects of the past sought only to seize Pharaoh's palace in order to install there the correct party. In this sense, they were insufficiently radical projects, as adorned as they might have been with the panoply of revolution. But even a radical project like Israel's experienced failure. That certainly merits our reflection, in order to help us not to repeat the same errors. In fact, a good part of the theology of the biblical writings is nothing more than a reflection on Israel's failure.

If we examine the diagnosis of the prophets, Israel's failure has two basic dimensions: the idolatry that substituted other gods for the God who had freed them from Egypt, and the internal injustices that kept Israel from presenting itself as an alternative for the other peoples. Here it is important to keep two things in mind. First, the criticisms of the prophets are directed primarily against the social injustices committed among the chosen people. The prophets are not surprised by the fact that social injustices are committed in Egypt, Assyria or Babylon. Such injustice was to be expected, because it corresponds to the basic logic of Adam-Babel, over against which Israel was to be an alternative. What is scandalous is that precisely the people called to be an alternative commits the same social injustices, thus nullifying the calling from God. Second, the prophets' criticism of social injustice cannot be separated from their criticism of idolatry, as if the former were a problem we still face while the latter was merely a "cultural" problem for ancient Israel and irrelevant to us. From the biblical viewpoint, as we have seen, injustice and idolatry are two sides of the same coin, precisely because both are rooted in the unbelief of "Adam," the human being.

This equation between idolatry and social injustice is something that can be observed clearly in the biblical story about the introduction of the monarchy. The egalitarian ethos of the Israelites is instinctively suspicious of all forms of the state, since they threaten to establish, in the midst of the chosen people, the palace of Pharaoh. The parable of Jotham expresses clearly this rejection: the desire to rule appears precisely in those persons who possess in themselves no redeeming quality and can find recognition only by doing harm to others (Judg 9:7-15). Nonetheless, the pressure from the Philistines progressively pushes the Israelites to desire, after two centuries without a state, a monarchy "like that of all the nations" (1 Sam 8:5). Obviously the desire to be like the other peoples makes it impossible for Israel to be an alternative. The prophet Samuel, in the name of YHWH, reluctantly accepts this desire of the people, but does not fail to warn about its dangers. The introduction of the monarchy means *both* a rejection of God, who thus ceases to reign directly over his people, *and* the introduction of social inequalities into the chosen people (1 Sam 8:1-22). In fact, the deuteronomical history presents the kings of Israel and Judah as the ones principally responsible both for idolatry and for social injustices. It is the introduction of the monarchy that leads not only to the division of the chosen people into two states, but also to the definitive collapse of both states before the great empires of Assyria and Babylon.

Of course, the experience of monarchy left Israel not only with a bad taste in its mouth, but also with certain models on which to base their hope for the future. The exceptional reign of David, sinner but never idolater, helps to formulate a vision of a new type of leadership, in the figure of a "son of David." Above all, however, the evil rule of the kings of Israel and Judah brings about the formulation of the desire that one day, in the future, God himself will again reign directly over his people. That is what is expressed, for example, in the oracle of the prophet Ezekiel:

> My sheep have become a prey, and my sheep have become food for all the wild beasts, since there was no shepherd; and because my shepherds have not searched for my sheep, but the shepherds have fed themselves, and have not fed my sheep . . . Thus says YHWH: Behold I, I myself will search for my sheep, and will seek them out . . . I will seek the lost, and I will bring back the strayed, and I will bind up the crippled, and I will strengthen the weak; but the fat and the strong I will destroy; I will feed them with justice . . . And I will set over them one shepherd, my servant David, and he shall feed them: he shall feed them and be their shepherd. And I, YHWH, will be their God, and my servant David shall be prince among them. (Ez 34:8,11,16,23-4)

The idea of a "reign of God" does not express simply a universal utopia of justice, much less a design for some new type of state, but above all the hope that God himself will reign over his people through his Messiah, thus establishing a new justice. For that reason it is above all a "reign" (*mlkt, basileía*) and not merely a "kingdom" of God.

In some passages, the Old Testament analyzes in greater detail the reasons for Israel's failure as an alternative society, and this analysis will be completed finally by the New Testament. According to certain texts, the problem does not consist only in Israel's repeated infidelity to God's plan, as expressed in the Torah. There is something in the people of Israel, harder to remove than the spots on the skin of a leopard, that always inclines her toward evil. The problem is ultimately in the heart of the human being, which must be changed, because without this change it is impossible to realize justice (Ez 11:19; 18:31; 36:26). Of course, the law of God, as an instruction for living in justice, does not by itself change the heart of the human being. The human being can continue to live with the "Adamic" logic of self-justification. Indeed, the law itself can be utilized for self-justification through fulfilling its precepts. Even though the law is a gift of God, the human being can use it to present himself as just, with a justice gained by his own effort. By this logic the apparent justice is nothing more than a more radical injustice: "We have all become like one who is unclean, and all our righteous deeds are like a polluted garment" (Is 64:6).

Paul will state later that the law, though good, was used by sin (Rom 7:7-25). And in the Acts of the Apostles we are told expressly that the forgiveness of sins and true justice could not be attained by means of the law of Moses (Acts 13:38-39). In fact, even the Old Testament makes explicit the inadequacy of the law of Moses to give life to the people (Ez 20:25) and the need for a new covenant: "Behold, the days are coming, says YHWH, when I will make a new covenant with the house of Israel and the house of Judah, not like the covenant which I made with their fathers when I took them out of the land of Egypt . . . I will put my law within them, and I will write it upon their hearts; and I will be their God, and they shall be my people" (Jer 31:31,33).

From this viewpoint, the realization of justice ceases to be limited to the memory of God's actions in the past and includes also the hope for God's action in the future. Faith, in this sense, is not only fidelity to the way initiated by the ancestors. It also includes hope in the future that God has already prepared for his people, despite their sins. If faith was necessary in the past to initiate the rupture with the established systems, what is requested now of the Israelite is to trust in the God of history and not in the empires that promise salvation from the threat of other empires. It is precisely faith in God that can ensure the political independence of the chosen people. Without that faith, the people cannot survive (Is 7:9). In the face of the bestial reality of empires that follow one upon the other, the believing Israelites hope for the beginning of God's reign over his people, the people of the saints of the Most High, and the final destruction of those empires (Dan 7:1-28).

Neither the need for a new covenant nor the transfer of hope to the future signified, however, a suspension of the fundamental strategy by which God will bring justice to humanity. The chosen people will preserve, even in the future, its function of being an alternative society toward which all the nations will feel themselves drawn. The idea of a pilgrimage of the nations to Mount Zion expresses nicely the gravitational pull that a restored Israel will exercise upon all humanity (Zeph 3:9-10). But this pilgrimage requires the renewal of the chosen people, the expulsion of the "proudly exultant ones" who have oppressed them, leaving only a humble remnant, in which there will be no injustice (Zeph 3:11-12). Only then will become possible the definitive gathering together of Israel and the fulfillment of its function with regard to all the peoples of the earth (Zeph 3:20). The faith of Israel is therefore reformulated thus:

> It shall come to pass in the latter days that the mountain of the house of YHWH shall be established as the highest of the mountains, and shall be raised above the hills; and all the nations shall flow to it, and many peoples shall come, and say: "Come, let us go up to the mountain of YHWH, to the house of the God of Jacob; that he may teach us his ways and that we may walk in his paths." For out of Zion shall go forth the law, and the word of the Lord from Jerusalem. He shall judge between the nations, and shall decide for many peoples; and they shall beat their swords into ploughshares, and their spears into pruning hooks; nation shall not lift up sword against nation, neither shall they learn war any more. (Is 2:2-4; cf. Mic 4:1-5)

"WILL NOT GOD VINDICATE HIS ELECT?"

The claim that justice will be realized in the future does not mean that justice will never be realized. Jesus of Nazareth appears in the history of Israel proclaiming the good news that God's reign has drawn near, has reached us and is already among us (Mt 3:2, 12:28; Lk 17:21).

Nevertheless, Jesus shuns being proclaimed king (Jn 6:15). We have already seen how in the Old Testament there appears a certain ambiguity with respect to the institution of the state. On the one hand, the monarchy is a possibility foreseen by the law; on the other, the institution of the state is accompanied by grave warnings from Samuel. Once the monarchy collapses after the disaster of the year 587 B.C., the restoration of Israel, as presented in the books of Ezekiel, Esdras and Nehemiah, does not seem to foresee the reappearance of an independent state, but provides only for the existence of an autonomous religious zone centered on the temple. That does not prevent the Jews from honoring figures like Joseph, Daniel or Esther, who fulfilled important roles in the empires of their day: not converting these empires into models of God's reign, but working to ensure, from their political positions, the survival of the chosen people. Despite Israel's ambiguous relationship with the monarchy, the forced imposition of Hellenistic culture gave rise to the guerrilla struggles of the Maccabeans, resulting in the installation of a new independent monarchy. It was obvious, however, that this monarchy could in no way present itself as the realization of the messianic hopes of Israel. In fact, the dynasty of the Maccabeans and their Hasmonean successors ends, as often happens with many "liberator" regimes, with some very distasteful characters, such as Herod.

In the time of Jesus and immediately following, various groups could still think that the people of God needed, for their survival and for the realization of their mission in history, the existence of state institutions, either in the form of a "realistic" coexistence with the Roman Empire (Sadducees) or in the form of a new revolution like that of the Maccabees (what the Zealots would end up advocating). Other groups, such as the Pharisees or the Essenes, preferred the idea of the stateless existence of the people of God, either through synagogal communities (Pharisees) or monastic separation (Qumran). Certainly Jesus did not expect a state-like realization of God's reign, for he is quite conscious that the existence of the state is linked to domination and oppression: "The rulers of the Gentiles lord it over them, and their great men exercise authority over them. It shall not be so among you" (Mt 20:25-26). Still, Jesus proposes something more radical than a simple synagogal existence or monastic retreat. Jesus wants a more radical transformation of the people of God.

The rejection of a political path does not signify, therefore, any spiritualism on Jesus' part, as can be observed in the accounts of the feeding of the multitudes (Mk 6:30-44; 8:1-10 and parallels). The story of the feeding of the Jewish multitude is situated after the murder of John the Baptist by Herod and presents Jesus with the apostles "in a lonely place" (Mk 6:31), a probable allusion to the situation of the Exodus. A multitude of people follow them, and Jesus has compassion on them and begins to teach them "because they were like sheep without a shepherd" (Mk 6:34). At the end of the day, the disciples feel no solidarity with the multitude and say to Jesus: "Send them away to go into the surrounding country and villages and buy themselves something to eat" (Mk 6:36). This would be a typically ecclesiastical reaction: the community of Jesus' disciples can provide a spiritual service to the multitudes, but the "material" aspects do not concern the church. The answer of Jesus contradicts this mentality head-on: "You give them something to eat" (Mk 6:37). Solving the material problem of the multitudes is a task proper to the disciples of Jesus. Obviously Jesus is not introducing any novelty into the Jewish faith. The center of faith in the Old Testament includes God's resolution of the material situation of the people enslaved in Egypt, by forming a new community in which there were not to be repeated the injustices experienced under the empire.

Nevertheless, the disciples have not understood fully what Jesus wants. In the face of the claim that the people must "buy" their food, Jesus has told them to "give": "You give them something to eat" (Mk 6:37). The disciples are still immersed in the logic of the prevailing economic system, including the logic of the Roman state. This immersion in the logic of the system includes, of course, the disciples' understanding of their own role, according to which they have to become mediators between the prevailing system and the needs of the people. This obviously supposes paternalism or some other type of vertical relationship between the disciples and the multitudes. In more recent times the disciples might perhaps have said: "Do you want us to found an NGO in order to feed these people?" Or maybe: "Do you want us to organize these people into a trade union, or a political party, so that they can lay claim before Herod to their right to be well-fed?" The disciples not only follow the logic of money, but also the logic of power. In reality, they are not two distinct logics: money is a quantification, ever more exact, of power.

Jesus' answer to the disciples' question breaks with such logic. Jesus simply asks them: "How many loaves have you? Go and see" (Mk 6:38). Here is the new logic that Christ unveils: It wasn't that the disciples were to buy food for the people. It wasn't that they were to put themselves over and above the multitude, making themselves their benefactors (Lk 22:25). Neither was it that the disciples were to found an NGO or that they should try to gain power in Herod's palace in order thus to feed the multitude. Jesus' proposal is more radical: the disciples are to open their own bags and share what they have. There is no need to go and buy in any nearby village, nor is there need to wait for political circumstances to change. From this very moment there becomes possible a different society, an alternative economic system, one that begins among those who are ready to share what they have, reclining on the green grass around Jesus (Mk 6:39-41). Eating in a reclining position was proper to free persons, not to those dependent on beneficent masters. Now all are equal. The green grass is a sign of abundance. The blessing of Jesus indicates that the new society is possible only by the grace of the liberator God, who begins to reign over his disciples. The twelve baskets of leftovers indicate that the foodstuffs which are shared apart from the system's logic are sufficient to feed Israel. The second account of the feeding of the multitudes will show that this logic is also possible for the pagans who join themselves to the community of Jesus (Mk 8:1-10).

In this way Jesus renews and radicalizes the justice project of Exodus. He renews it, because he calls anew for the formation of an alternative society. He radicalizes it, because he is conscious that the formation of a new community is possible only by means of an attachment to his own person which enables the disciple to abandon the securities which come from economic, family and religious positions (Mt 10:37-39). The episodes around the so-called "young rich man" demonstrate this well. We are not dealing here with a call to the religious life, but with the inadequacy of the law of Moses to form the new society (Mk 10:17-20). Only detachment from one's own possessions and the following of Jesus make possible entrance into the new community, over which God exercises his reign (Mk 10:21-25). Of course, rich people have problems entering into this new logic, but so also do those who claim to have left all to follow Christ. As in the Exodus, only the gratuitous initiative of God makes possible the creation of a new reality in history: what is not possible for human beings is possible for God (Mk 10:26-27). Nevertheless, the difficult rupture with the bonds of the system does not leave the persons alone before God, but gives birth to a new community, in which all kinds of human relationships are refounded, except those of a paternal type (Mk 10:28-31; Mt 23:9). The challenge which this supposes for the system means that the new community will be subjected to persecutions (Mk 10:30-34). The difficulty of entering into this new logic is shown in the petition of the sons of Zebedee, who want to reproduce in the new community the political structures of the established system (Mk 10:35-45). Faith must make possible a new way of seeing things, freeing us from blindness (Mk 10:46-52). Without this faith there is no new community, and therefore there is no justice and no reign of God.

From this point of view both Jesus' rejection of kingship and his attitude toward the Roman Empire turn out to be perfectly comprehensible. When Jesus says "Render to Caesar the things that are Caesar's, and to God the things that are God's" (Mk 12:17), he is not simply establishing a distinction between the political and the spiritual. First of all, Jesus, in asking them for a Roman coin, has already demonstrated the hypocrisy of the leaders of Israel: not only the religious hypocrisy in possessing a coin with the idolatrous image of the divinized emperor, but also the economic hypocrisy of questioning the payment of taxes to the invading power even while they participate in and benefit from the economic system which that power guarantees. Second, Jesus does not say simply "render" or "give" to Caesar what belongs to him, but "return it to him" (*apódote*). It is not a question of declaring that the disciple has two types of obligation, one to Caesar and one to God, as might be deduced from the verb "render." It is a question of returning to Caesar what belongs to him, and this involves returning all the denarii. What Jesus seeks to establish is a new community, free of the logic of the system, one that involves economic independence. Returning to God what belongs to God, for its part, does not mean fulfilling certain religious obligations. That is neither the biblical idea nor that of Jesus' hearers. From the biblical viewpoint, to God belong not only the land and all that it contains (Ps 24:1), but also, in a special way, the people of

Israel, taken out from among other peoples in order to become God's very own people (Ex 6:7). In this way, Jesus not only recalls God's original project for his people, which Jesus is now renewing and radicalizing, but also points out the inability of the Jewish leaders themselves to allow Israel to be the true people of God. The false shepherds must return the people to God.

In order to achieve this restoration, it is not enough to retreat to the monasteries in the desert. But neither is there sense in seeking political power by means of violence. Quite the contrary: Jesus calls for a radical renunciation of violence, to the point of requiring love for one's enemies (Mt 5:38-48). The examples of Jesus are quite concrete and include explicit reference to the Roman custom of obliging occupied peoples to carry soldiers' equipment for the distance of one mile (Mt 5:41). Indeed, the use of violence to gain power is in no way an alternative to the logic prevailing in the world. If the defense of the alternative society requires one to do the same as the pagans do, that defense ceases to be sensible, because it ceases to be an alternative. It does no more than confirm the unstoppable logic of violence, which the states seek to monopolize but not suppress (Mt 26:52). For that very reason the alternative society of Jesus is not a state-like society, nor is the reign of God like any kingdom of this world. But it is a real reign, in the midst of history, and precisely for that reason presents a challenge to the states of this world. Indeed, the promises of peace that the prophets had announced for the messianic reign must begin to be put into practice starting now, because the messianic reign, from Jesus' viewpoint, is not for the future, but has already begun. The non-violence of Jesus is not simply an immediate strategy, but is the attitude that is most coherent with the announcement that the reign of God has already begun.

Nonetheless, Jesus dies executed by the state authorities, Jewish and Roman, in Jerusalem. In view of this execution, it might be thought that God's project has failed, that God has not really initiated his reign of justice. Apparently God has not heard the petitions of Jesus in the garden, nor has he vindicated his elect, who cry to him day and night (Lk 18:7). The faith of the Christian community, however, will proclaim quite the contrary: in Christ the realization of justice in this world has become possible in a most unusual way.

"THE JUSTICE WHICH IS BY FAITH"

From the viewpoint of the first Christian communities, the death of Christ on the cross forms part of the good news: the good news that now true justice is really possible, independently of the law of Moses (Rom 3:31). This belief has ordinarily been understood in more individualistic terms and has frequently referred to the hereafter. However, the New Testament writers intend to say quite the opposite: the New Testament proclaims that what the law of Israel could not accomplish is now possible through Jesus Christ. As we saw, what the law of Israel sought was precisely to constitute a distinct people in which justice would be practiced, in order thus to fascinate and attract toward itself all the peoples of the earth. For that very reason, the justice of which the New Testament speaks is not primarily an ethical requirement, but a good news: the good news that the justice of God has been definitively revealed in Christ (Rom 1:16-17). Furthermore, that justice is not for the other world, but has begun already in history and is being practiced now in the Christian communities (Rom 5:17).

God's justice is realized in the Christian communities, and not in the Roman or Jewish state, because the justice of which the New Testament speaks is possible only through faith. To illustrate this Paul refers at times to the story of "Adam": the logic proper to Adam has been canceled by Christ, the new Adam (1 Cor 15:45). The logic proper to "Adam," that is, the logic proper to the human being apart from faith, is the logic of self-justification. It is the pretension of justifying oneself by the results of one's own actions. From this viewpoint, God appears as the one who assures that each person will receive the merited result of his or her actions. This not only implies that the good are rewarded and the evil punished; it also implies that those who are apparently punished are punished because they have done something wrong. It is the problem with which Job was confronted. With Christ this logic is definitively negated, because Christ was apparently abandoned and punished by God (Gal 3:13; 2 Cor 5:21). Nevertheless, God was in Christ, reconciling the world to himself (2 Cor 5:19), and precisely for that reason death could not restrain Jesus. This presence of God in Jesus crucified means not only that God has entered into solidarity with all the victims of history, with all those who are apparently abandoned by God; but also means that God has nullified the idea of a correspondence between our actions and their results, and thereby rejected our vain pretensions to justify ourselves by the results of our actions. At the same time, God's solidarity includes the victory already achieved by Christ over all the economic, political and religious powers that, like the serpent, seek to assure us of a correspondence between our actions and their results: God "canceled the bond which stood against us with its legal demands; this he set aside, nailing it to the cross. He disarmed the principalities and powers and made a public example of them, triumphing over them in him" (Col 2:14-15).

What this means is that God has granted us justification gratuitously: not as the result of our efforts, but by faith (Rom 3:28). God's justice consists in having given us faith, and faith gains for us justice. This justice is not something interior or spiritual; it is certainly justice toward God, but it is also social justice, which now is realized in the Christian communities. What Israel could not attain—the elimination of poverty (Deut 15:4)—the Christian communities can attain when they are built upon faith (Acts 4:34). The need for faith resides precisely in the fact that, if we do not trust that God has gratuitously declared us just in Christ, thus rendering useless the pretension of justifying ourselves as a result of our actions, then we will necessarily continue to seek to justify ourselves. And if we continue to seek to justify ourselves, we will continue to introduce into the world the consequences of the Adamic pretension of experiencing the results of our own actions. We will continue to be afraid of God, we will continue to manipulate other people to avoid our own responsibility, we will continue to envy others, we will continue to oppress others to gain admiration or power, and we will most definitely construct in history new towers of Babel. Earth will be the scene of our thirst for production, and the ultimate result of our life will be death.

By contrast, if we trust that Christ, by his life, death and resurrection, has annulled the law of self-justification, we are able to renounce the pretension of power and prestige. We no longer have to fear a God who judges our output, but rather can rest in him and confidently call him *Abba*, Father (Rom 8:15). We will not have to distrust our neighbor as our possible judge and oppressor, but rather as Christians we will be able to consider ourselves brothers and sisters, members of a family of equals, a family in which all patriarchal paternalism disappears. The goods of the earth will no longer be at the service of a mad race for production, but will be able to be enjoyed again as gratuitous gifts that can be shared in community. The differences of gender will no longer need to be understood in terms of domination or competition, but rather in terms of reconciled complementarity. Death itself will have lost its sting (1 Cor 15:55), because it no longer threatens us as the final result of all our efforts. The injustice engendered by "Adam's" unbelief is now replaced by the justice made possible by the faith of Christ, author of our own faith (Heb 12:2). For that very reason, biblical justice is indissolubly united to faith. It is not the justice of general ethical obligations, but a new justice. It is no longer one's own justice, but the justice which comes from the faith of Christ, the justice which is of God through faith (Phil 3:9).

The New Testament affirms the possibility of realizing social justice in the communities that arise from faith (Acts 2:42-46; 4:32-37). It is not a matter of simply satisfying material needs, but of a whole new way of life, in which peace, justice and human happiness are realized (Rom 14:17). This is not the result of our own efforts, but is a fruit of the Spirit, precisely because, if faith were our work, we would be able to boast of it, and we would continue in the same logic of Adam (Eph 2:8-9). What we know historically of the Christian communities of the first three centuries is that in fact they practiced, within certain limitations, a form of alternative life in which not only was poverty overcome, but the differences deriving from gender and social status were reduced or eliminated. That was not due to the Christian communities' seeking to conquer the palace of the Roman emperor, or that of Herod or Caiaphas, in order to bring about social reforms from there later. The attractive and dangerous aspect of the Christian communities consisted in the fact that they actually (not just ideally), from the base (not from presidential palaces) and in the present (not as future promise), practiced the new justice and proclaimed that they were under a new sovereignty, the sovereignty of Christ, who in this way was exercising now in history the reign of God (Acts 17:6-8). The prayer of Christians for the authorities has precisely this meaning: it asks that the authorities allow them to practice their new form of alternative life (1 Tim 2:1-2). Precisely because justice was a reality, Christian apologetes such as Justin could state, in response to Judaism, that there were concrete proofs that the Messiah had already come, and that that Messiah was Jesus. The prophetic promises for the messianic era, according to which violence and injustice were to disappear (Isa 11:1-9), were being realized already in the Christian communities.

THE PRESENT TIME OF JUSTICE

If we now try to apply these biblical teachings to the present, we must begin by recognizing that all too frequently Christians continue to believe that the key to achieving social justice lies in the seizure of Pharaoh's palace by an appropriate political group. No doubt it is important to know who actually holds political power in any moment of history. The Pharaoh who welcomed Joseph and his brothers is very different from the Pharaoh (Rameses II) who imposed harsh slavery on the Israelites. Not all the emperors behaved the same way with regard to the challenge of the Christian communities. This fact alone would suffice to justify a profound interest in politics on the part of Christians. Obviously, we are not talking about a sectarian or selfish interest, as might happen, for example, when the clergy in some churches defend their own economic interests or their own educational institutions. What is at stake is something very different: namely, that the Christian communities, when they are true churches, constitute by themselves the first fruits of a new humanity, the very place where God's justice begins to break into history. In this sense, concern for the transformation of all humanity requires concern for the historical viability of communities in which there have already begun to exist the innovations proper to the messianic era. If Christians aspire to realize justice in history, they must guarantee the possibility that now, in our world, there be a truly visible alternative to the grave injustices that plague our society.

This means, then, that the Joseph/Daniel/Esther model continues to be a valid reference point for considering the possible political functions of believers. In the New Testament as well there appears a believer who holds a public office in his city (Rom 16:23).

Nevertheless, we should understand correctly the meaning of these political functions. When they have a theological meaning beyond the simple employment involved, this consists precisely in the service that can be rendered from different political posts to the survival of the chosen people of God. This service is critical precisely because this people, as an alternative society, is almost constantly persecuted by the bestial empires that feel threatened by the mere existence of the chosen people (Dan 7:15-28). Of course, such public posts exist because of interests proper to the state in question, and this involves the possibility of their offering great services to the old society, as is shown for example in the political achievement of Joseph in Egypt. Christian love is directed to all, even while the alternative community is not made up of all (Lk 10:25-37; Gal 6:10). By contrast, what directly contradicts the biblical testimony is the naive, and basically conservative, tendency to think that political changes made from imperial palaces might constitute the beginning of the reign of God in history. The tendency is naive because it ignores the constitutively violent nature of every state; it is conservative because it forsakes the truly radical changes, thus consolidating the political system, instead of affirming, like Daniel, its radical insolvency (Dan 2:37-45). Besides, it is not to be forgotten that the exercise of such political functions ordinarily requires behavior that is hardly compatible with exclusive fidelity to the Christian God. The powerful frequently feel inclined to guarantee the loyalty of their collaborators by requiring of them not only oaths, but also an idolatrous allegiance to their own person. The believer who takes on public responsibilities without renouncing his or her faith should not forget the danger of ending up in the lions' den, or at least, like Esther, in the harem of the emperor.

The decisive scene of God's action is elsewhere: in those communities that allow God to reign and be Lord over them, driving out all idols and beginning now a new society. This is the true "politics": the formation of assemblies (*ekklesíai*) of free persons in which economic and social differences disappear. Within the Christian church, as a new convocation of Israel (*qahal*)—in contrast to the assemblies of the Greek *polis*—women and slaves took active part, thus showing the possibility of a new society. Unfortunately, many religious leaders today prefer to dedicate their energies to the established *polis*, and not to the service of alternative communities. The absurd extreme takes place when religious leaders preach to the powerful that they must organize their societies in a different way, in the absence of Christian communities that can demonstrate that it is actually possible, by the grace of God, to live in another way. The burn-out of many base communities has its ultimate cause in this fatal imbalance. In a certain way, religious leaders find it easier to denounce the irresponsibility of the powerful than to see how many loaves they themselves have in their own bags, not to be handed out paternalistically, but to be placed at the disposition of all in a banquet of equals. In the gospel, much more important than the "announcing and denouncing" is the primary and decisive *renouncing* of possessions. For that very reason, the renunciation of possessions is not preached primarily to Herod or Caesar Augustus, but is required simply and plainly of the disciple who wants to follow Christ and form part of his community.

The great question regarding justice has to do with the willingness of present-day Christians to allow the Spirit to form messianic communities that demonstrate the possibility of an alternative to the system. In fact, whenever the Spirit acts in the churches, more or less satisfactory communities of this type appear, despite the fact that the stridency of popular religious culture is often distasteful to theologians. Such communities have always existed in the history of the Christian church, in all denominations. Nevertheless, a stubborn Constantinianism continues to make many believe that the place *par excellence* for social change can only be society as a whole. Since the fourth century, many have held the idea that all society is, or should be, in some way and almost naturally, Christian. In Latin America, the conquest meant a brutal continuation of this Constantinianism, so that many people even in the twentieth century continue to speak of a "Christian continent," despite the flagrant injustices, despite the evangelization frequently only imposed and apparent, despite the progressive secularization and despite the profound religious divisions. However, continents are not Christian: only persons and communities are. In the Constantinian mentality, since all are presumably Christian, all form part of God's people, and all are called to be transformed into a society modeled on the Exodus and the gospel. This way of thinking, although it may inspire some cosmetic improvement in the system, is powerless to present truly radical alternatives to the prevailing capitalist civilization. Society as a whole cannot be governed by ideals that require the demise of the system and which are therefore possible only through the freedom of faith. When all are falsely made out to be Christians, the only remedy is to lower the radical requirements of Christianity, in order to convert it into a social ethic applicable to all. In the end the only thing that is asked is that the powerful, like Hammurabi, be mindful of the orphan and the widow. In this schema there is room for moments of confrontation between throne and altar, but such episodes will necessarily be brief, because both the throne and the altar will continue to be part of a social system into which no newness has been introduced. Their common interests, from education to public ceremonies, will always have them returning to sit together at the same table.

Faith and justice are a transforming newness only where they are really acting forces, where they are demonstrating, by means of the existence of alternative communities, the possibility of another form of life. There is not much sense in asking Pharaoh, Herod or Caiaphas to commit themselves to social justice, even while Christians continue to live in institutions that share the same logic and the same forms of government that prevail in the social system as a whole. A struggle for justice realized in this way could only propose, with the bitterness of the impossible, certain general ethical requirements, but not a true alternative. In a phase of world capitalism such as the one we are presently enduring, real and visible alternatives are more necessary than ever; simple, moralizing invocations of justice are not sufficient. Even people of a secular mindset who are seeking alternatives to the dominant system concur in affirming the need to establish new economic forms from the grassroots. From a Christian perspective, this is precisely what faith makes possible. Christians can give the world the good news that another way of life is already possible, and is already at work in history. For that very reason, many churches and communities are in need of profound conversion, for they are burdened with the same authoritarian and unequal logic as the most conservative groups in society, or as those groups which pose as progressive, but are no longer seen by anybody as a true alternative, because they do not practice justice within themselves.

In a world as disillusioned as ours is, in a world where, as Bishop Pedro Casaldaliga used to say, half the population dies of hunger and the other from the fear of death, it is more necessary than ever to present real alternatives, and not engage only in general ethical discourses or rivalries for power. Neither Herod nor Caiaphas, neither Spartacus nor Barabbas nor any multinational Pharaoh is going to move the world significantly toward justice. The world changes only where the death and resurrection of Christ truly initiate an alternative way of life, one capable of showing up the falsity of the dominant system and demonstrating the viability of different human relationships. The appearance of small-time Pharaohs, of left-leaning priest-kings, is not a "good news" that destabilizes the system or that attracts poor people toward it. What changes the world in an effective manner is the appearance of communities in which, by faith, new relations of justice begin to be practiced. The good news is that these communities, despite the disobedience of Christians throughout history, have never disappeared completely, and that the Spirit keeps creating them wherever believers hear the word of life with open ears. The Exodus is taking place in the present time, and continues to be possible for Christians. At stake in all this is not only a project for social change, but something more radical still. Indeed, if the Messiah has really come, there must already exist in the world a different society. The most decisive alternative is not between left and right, between good Pharaohs and bad ones. The truly decisive alternative exists between the wall of lamentations and the joyous affirmation that the Messiah has already come and now reigns as Lord over his tiny people.

3

Matthew 25 and the Hope of the Poor

According to Ignacio Ellacuría, theology constitutes an "ideological moment of ecclesial praxis."[1] Though this statement should not be interpreted mechanistically, it confirms the relationship between many theological interpretations and the ecclesial praxis from which they arise and which they condition. In these pages I would like to ask about the relationship between the theological interpretations of Matthew 25:31-46 and their respective forms of social praxis. Of course, this question is by no means neutral, but is posed explicitly from a concrete point of view: that of ascertaining how the different theological interpretations of this text are capable of sustaining the hopes of Christians in the midst of the injustice which prevails in this world. As is known, the gospel text presents us with Jesus as a shepherd, who at the end of the day divides the "nations" into two groups ("sheeps" and "goats") and judges them with regard to the attitudes they have toward his "least brethren." After mentioning the hungry, the thirsty, foreigners, the naked, the sick and the imprisoned, Jesus says to them, both to the "just" and to the "accursed," that what they did to the least, they did to him as well.

For centuries the text has nourished the commitment of Christians to help the very poorest. In recent years the text has become an obligatory reference point for all Christians dedicated to the work of justice. It is not, however, a text that is easily interpreted,

---

A first version of this work was presented in the colloquium on "Christian Humanism" which took place in the Universidad Iberoamericana de México, in November 2000.

and all kinds of positions can be found among exegetes. There are two especially controversial points. First, there is the problem of determining who are the "nations" (*éthne*) whom Jesus judges. For some, these "nations" designate all the peoples of the earth,[2] while for others they designate specifically the "Gentiles," that is, the non-believing peoples, as opposed to the Christian group.[3] Matthew continues to employ the Hebrew distinction between the people of God (*'am*) and the other peoples (*goyim*). But this poses the further question of whether the Israel which has not accepted Jesus is considered in Matthew to be still part of the believing people, or rather to belong now to the sphere of "the peoples" and therefore to the sphere of universal mission.[4] Secondly, there is also debate about the identity of the "least brethren" or the most "insignificant" (*elákhistos*), those with whom Jesus identifies himself. For some they are the believers, precisely as siblings of Jesus,[5] while for others they are any poor person.[6]

We do not hope to resolve the exegetical problem here definitively, but we do seek to enter into its theological dimensions and to present an interpretation of the text on the basis of them. These theological dimensions are historically conditioned, of course, and can in turn influence the opinions of the exegetes themselves. Thus, for example, in a situation of Christendom, when the church identifies itself with society as a whole, the reference to non-Christian "nations" loses its meaning. For that reason it is not strange that Luther would still interpret the narrative of Matthew 25:31-46 as a judgment referring to what Christians do to other Christians. The text might otherwise have possibly lost all its meaning in medieval Christendom. Something very different can occur in the context of growing secularization and general disregard of ecclesiastical institutions. If in such circumstances it is thought that faith should in some way still be acceptable for the major part of society, the interpretation of Matthew 25:31-46 can be the very opposite: the parable could be referring simply to what anyone (believer or not) does with any needy person (believer or not). The decisive factor, at the defining hour of salvation, would be the ethical commitment to the least members of any society.

To approach an answer to these problems, we are going to understand these texts from what Gustavo Gutiérrez calls the "perspective of the poor." That is, we are going to take a particular theological interpretation of the text about the "judgment of the nations," and we are going to examine it in function of what this interpretation can mean for the poorest people. Concretely, we will ask about the hope of the poor, such as this might be articulated on the basis of the particular interpretation of this text. This of course requires some contact on the part of the theologian with the poor, and it also requires knowledge of what religious sociology tells us about popular faith.[7]

HOPE IN "HUMANIST CONSTANTINIANISM"

To simplify, we may distinguish the two interpretations mentioned above: one is "traditional Constantinianism," and the other is "humanist Constantinianism." Both interpretations can be called "Constantinian" in the sense that both seek a universalization of the essential contents of the Christian faith by making use of public powers. In the first case, Christians counted on Christian public powers (kings, emperors, princes) to impose, even violently, the (real or supposed) contents of Christianity on all society. In the second case, there is no pretension of imposing all the traditional contents of the Christian faith on the society as a whole. Religious pluralism is accepted, but there is an effort to have society as a whole conform to what is considered to be of the essence of the faith. In this case, what is of the essence of the faith would be defined precisely by Matthew 25:31-46, and would be nothing other than the "option for the poor." Christians, by using diverse political means, both peaceful and violent, would have to bring it about that the public powers transform the structures of a determined society for the benefit of the poorest.

From this perspective, the interpretation of Matthew 25:31-46 by "humanist Constantinianism" would be done in the following manner. The parable speaks for "all the nations," and this means all the peoples, believing or not, including therefore both Christians and Israel. All would appear before the judge, Jesus Christ. He would judge all humanity by a well-defined criterion: their behavior toward the neediest people of every kind. These needy people would be both believers and non-believers, because such a distinction would be completely irrelevant. The only relevant factor would be their situation of need. In the same way that the Samaritan took pity on the assaulted traveler (Lk 10:25-37), so also Matthew's text would establish as the definitive criterion for salvation the attitude of any person toward any other person in need, beyond all ethnic and religious distinctions. Since we are dealing precisely with a judgment, we are being told what is the most essential for Christian faith: our effective response to the need of others. However, unbelievers also respond to the needs of others, even to the point of giving their lives for them. Thus Christian practice (except for certain liturgical meetings) would not be distinguished from the practice of those non-believers who are committed to striving to relieve the sufferings of others. In trade unions, political parties or non-governmental organizations, the practice of believers and non-believers would be the same: the struggle for a better society, in which there is no poverty or oppression.

Without doubt there is much that is true and valuable in this interpretation of "humanist Constantinianism," which we here explain in only the most succinct and schematic way. Nonetheless, I would like to call attention to a critical point, which to me seems very important: namely, that the interpretation we have just explained *is directed primarily to people who are not poor but who have sufficient resources, power and time to be able to do something for the poor.* This interpretation can be directed to cultivated persons of the secularized societies of the West—or, why not say it, to a clergyperson whose living standard is not the same as that of the poor. In general, this interpretation is addressed to persons who are not poor, and it calls them to commit themselves to the poor. Comfortable Christians are told that Christ is among the most poor, awaiting our commitment to them. Non-believers are told that what Christianity ultimately expects of them is that they commit themselves to the poor, their faith being irrelevant to their salvation. In each case, the people appealed to are not the poor, but rather people who make an option for the poor. This is precisely the ambiguity, so often pointed out, that hides behind the expression "option for the poor."[8]

Let us now try to place ourselves within the perspective of the poor people, in order to inquire about how the interpretation given by "humanist Constantinianism" can affect their hopes. Anyone who has ever tried to explain this interpretation within a context of poverty will possibly know what I am referring to. Without any doubt, humanist Constantinianism has the merit of telling poor people, insofar as they are believers, that Christ is in the midst of them. From the viewpoint of the Christian faith, the identification of God with Christ implies a divine solidarity with all the condemned of the earth.[9] This central truth of the Christian faith is announced to the poor when the aforementioned interpretation of the gospel's last judgment scene is presented to them. Naturally this announcement is comprehensible for the poor people who are believers. For the poor people who are not believers of any religion, or for the millions of poor who belong to other religions, this affirmation of God's solidarity with them can appear perfectly incomprehensible. It is not unusual that in certain religions or secular ideologies poor people are seen as rejected by God, as sinners, or as culpable for their own poverty. That does not mean, of course, that there do not exist in some religions contrary affirmations as well.[10]

Let us rather adopt then the most favorable position and posit that the poor really are believers and do share in the affirmation that God is in radical solidarity with their fate. In the cross God has taken on the fate of the poor, so that solidarity with the poor becomes an encounter with God himself. As the book of Proverbs pointed out, "who lends to the poor lends to God himself" (Prov 19:17). These ancient texts acquire their full meaning from the identification of God with Christ. The solidarity of God can doubtless be a source of consolation for the poor. Our question, though, is not about consolation, but rather about hope. What hopes can this interpretation of the text awaken among the poor? The persons who suffer hunger, thirst, nakedness, sickness, uprooting or imprisonment place their hope in liberation from these situations which in general terms we can characterize as "poverty." Their hope cannot easily be satisfied by knowing that God is at their side. Neither does it suffice to have hope that is oriented exclusively to the great beyond. *The hope of the poor is to escape from their poverty.* And when the poor spell out their hopes religiously, that basic objective of their hope does not disappear.

So the interpretation of "humanist Constantinianism" seems not to provide more than a rudimentary source of hope for the poor. That source of hope *seems to be simply the commitment to help the poor made by those who are not poor but who nonetheless enter into solidarity with the situation of the poor.* Of course, these people can argue theoretically that it is the poor who must organize and themselves become the subjects of their own liberation, etc. However, in the interpretation of the text that we have given, the poor *are not properly subjects, but objects* toward whom the solidarity of the non-poor is directed. These latter can be well-off Christians, clergy or non-believers; they may advocate "structural change" and may head up trade unions, political parties or non-governmental organizations. To the extent that these people espouse certain social or political causes and have success in their struggles, to that extent the poor can have hope that social changes will take place that allow them to escape from poverty. These changes are no doubt important, and on occasions they even manage to get carried into practice . . .

Nevertheless, it is important to observe that within this perspective *the poor do not emerge from their position of dependency.* Their hope depends on the commitment of other people to them.[11] When the poor do not have a voice, then others become their spokespersons, as "the voice of those who have no voice." If the poor are to have any role in social change, it will primarily consist in supporting the initiatives that others have taken. No doubt, in the measure that these initiatives appear to be effective, many poor people can feel attracted to them. In fact, even the most despotic rulers, if they are able to promise and to bring about improvements that favor the poor, will find among them many admirers and followers. In this way some social changes can be achieved, but not an authentic transformation of society in its basic structures of domination. Society, even after the most costly revolutions, will continue to be divided into two groups: the beneficiaries and the benefactors. The primary hope of the beneficiaries will be for the existence and the effectiveness of the benefactors. It could even be insinuated that *the poor experience Christ's solidarity with them through the solidarity of the benefactors.* It is the supreme legitimization of a dependency that does not radically transform social structures.

If now, following the intuition of Ellacuría, we ask about the relationships between this interpretation of the text and its corresponding ecclesial praxis, we would have to say that the interpretations of "humanist Constantinianism" are proper to an ecclesial praxis characterized by the existence of great social differences in the interior of the respective church. The theological interpretation of "humanist Constantinianism" will be characteristic of ecclesial groups which, being well-off, have felt ethically challenged by these social differences and, in the name of the gospel, have undertaken diverse tasks of service to the poor. These tasks can be of very different types, from the most typically political to various forms of solidarity in non-governmental organizations. The "humanist Constantinian" interpretation of the text implies that people who are affluent, and yet socially conscious, will be committed, sometimes heroically, to the poorest people of their society. But it does not imply a change in the social relationships within the church itself. The well-off groups, even though they are socially conscious and active, will continue to belong to a different class from the poor to whom they direct their helpful efforts. The social differences between the poor and their benefactors will not disappear. No social newness will have appeared in history.

THE GOSPEL OF MATTHEW

Let us see if there is another possible reading of Matthew 25:31-46 which, while remaining true to the biblical text, allows us also to describe a hope in which the poor are not primarily the object of solidarity, but above all the subjects of their own destiny. To do this we must situate the passage in a wider context, drawing from it some hints for understanding how the final judgment scene in Matthew points toward a much more radical hope. Although the interpretation we present here is based on the work of exegetes, I have found it spontaneously expressed also in various pentecostal communities with popular roots.

The Social Context of Matthew

As is known, Matthew's Gospel comes from a Judeo-Christian context which, while trying to preserve the heritage of Israel, is still open to the Gentile church and the preaching of the Gospel to the whole world.[12] The community of Matthew already understands itself as *ekklesía* (Mt 16:18; 18:17), different from the synagogue, and as the true heir of the promises made to Israel, which have been fulfilled in Jesus Christ. Since the Gospel of Matthew presupposes the destruction of Jerusalem by Roman troops, its date of composition must be placed after the year 70. Traditionally it has been suggested that the gospel could have been written in Syria, where a good number of Jews and Christians were living. Many recent authors, however, suggest that the gospel was composed in Palestine itself, since Matthew seems to assume a permanent critical dialogue with the authority of "the wise" (the "scribes and Pharisees"), that is, with the new leaders of Judaism after the catastrophic destruction of the temple by the Romans. Matthew's fluent Greek would be no obstacle to this localization, since it was common in some circles of Hellenistic Jews in Palestine.[13]

The community of Matthew is possibly located in an urban context. In contrast with the Gospel of Mark, which mentions the word "city" (*pólis*) only eight times, the Gospel of Matthew mentions it 27 times; such frequency supposes an urban context for his community, although not one completely separated from the rural milieu. Such a context is confirmed by several mentions of the marketplace (Mt 11:16; 20:3) and by the trades in which people are employed (Mt 22:5). Possibly, there were some members of the more affluent classes, or even of the elite, in Matthew's community. Joseph of Arimathea, who in the Gospel of Mark is a "prominent member of the Council, who was himself waiting for the reign of God" (Mk 15:43), is described in the Gospel of Matthew as "rich" and as a "disciple" (Mt 27:57). In the Gospel of Matthew, differently from Mark, we also find more detailed mention of the Jewish elite and of the affluent classes: elders, Sadducees, Pharisees, scribes, and also publicans and officials of the Roman army. This does not mean that all these persons were part of Matthew's community, but it does mean that his gospel was written in a context where a more differentiated attention was paid to those social groups. Nevertheless, the majority of the members of Matthew's community belonged to the lower classes. Especially noteworthy, compared to the Gospel of Mark, is the frequent mention of slaves (*doûlos*) and servants (*paîs*).[14] Also noteworthy, in comparison with Mark, is the mention of prostitutes as persons who believe in the preaching of John and therefore enter into the reign of God before the religious and civil leaders (Mt 21:31-32). Thus we have a community composed of a majority of persons who come from the lower classes, together with some members who come from the affluent classes. Because of their acceptance of the Christian message, the community occupies a marginal position with respect to society as a whole.[15]

The New People of God

To understand the way that the evangelist Matthew responds to the problem of poverty, we must first understand the general perspective of his work. Matthew insists that in Jesus, the promises of Scripture have been fulfilled.[16] This viewpoint marks a radical difference between the communities that have accepted the Messiah and the leaders of official Judaism, who have rejected and executed Jesus. The parable of the murderous vineyard tenants is directed primarily against the leaders of Israel (Mt 21:23, 33-45). While the vineyard is a symbol of Israel (Is 5:1-7), the tenants of the vineyard represent its leaders.[17] The parable indicates that these leaders have sought to seize for themselves the fruits of the vineyard instead of handing them over to the rightful owner, who is none other than God.[18] This usurpation has reached the point of murdering the son of the vineyard's owner. Therefore, the vineyard will be taken away from them and will be handed over to a people which is not yet believing (*éthnos*), but which will offer the Lord the fruits of the harvest. In this way God will again reign over the vineyard, which is nothing but the original Israel, and will thus regain the fruits which belonged to him originally.[19]

The renewed establishment of the people of God requires the repetition of Israel's own foundational events. As Pharaoh once sought to destroy the Israelites by killing the male newborns, in the same way Herod appears on the scene killing innocent children in order to do away with Jesus. Like the patriarch with the same name, Joseph is now the father of Jesus who saves his family by taking them to Egypt. Matthew comments on these events by quoting a verse from the prophet Hosea: "Out of Egypt I have called my son" (Hos 11:1). Now, however, it is the land of Israel which fulfills the role of Egypt, because Israel has become a place of slavery and oppression. The flight from the oppressors is now a flight toward Egypt, and later the displaced settle, not in Judea, where Herod's son reigns, but in "Galilee of the Gentiles" (Mt 4:15). The important factor, in any case, is that Jesus appears holding the place of Israel as "son of God." The renewal of Israel as a new people of God begins precisely with Jesus.[20] As Moses on the mountain once transmitted the law of God to his people, now also Jesus, on a mountain, proclaims the beatitudes as the magna carta of the messianic Israel which is gathered around Jesus (Mt 4:25-8:1).

The Israel of the Poor

The Recipients of the Good News

The beatitudes of Jesus are directed first of all to the poor, who are proclaimed especially blessed, along with those who suffer, those who are humiliated and those who hunger and thirst for justice (Mt 5:3-6). The situation of the poor is going to change radically with the arrival of the reign of God. God is going to take possession again of his own people, re-establishing the original sense of Israel as a people among whom there should be no poor (Deut 15:4). Just as the original Israel was formed from those who were oppressed in Egypt, among whom were found not only the descendents of Jacob-Israel but also many other exploited persons (Ex 12:38),[21] so also the Israel renewed by the Messiah comprises the poorest people of every provenance. The election of Israel did not mean, however—either then or now—permanent poverty, but quite the contrary. What was sought in the Exodus was the formation of a different people, among whom there would be neither poverty nor exploitation. In the same way, poverty and oppression will also disappear in the messianic Israel of Jesus. It is a matter of visible transformations, which Jesus can present as good news for the poor (Mt 11:5).

In what do these transformations consist? Is it just a matter of the therapeutic activity of Jesus, who is able to restore sight to the blind and hearing to the deaf? Or is it simply a spiritual type of news, referring more to the salvation of our souls? In such cases, it would be hard to see why the gospel should be good news for the poor as such. The truth is that Matthew, like all of early Christianity, counts on real transformations in the lives of the poor. That is what is expressed, for example, in the story of the feeding of the multitude, recounted in all four gospels.[22] Matthew states plainly that the feeding of the multitudes is a task of the disciples (Mt 14:16). In constrast to what happens in the Gospel of Mark, where the disciples understand this task in a paternalist way (Mk 6:37), in the Gospel of Matthew the disciples already see quite clearly how Jesus wants the multitudes to be fed: by means of sharing. The disciples must place everything they have at the disposal of the crowds, gathered around Jesus for the banquet. Matthew, more clearly than Mark, emphasizes the disciples' inability to feed the masses with the few food items in their possession (Mt 14:17). Indeed, sharing is effective only when a new community is established, one in which no one keeps anything for himself or herself. Thus Matthew indicates, as did the book of Exodus previously, that the new society is possible only as the miracle of a God who transforms the desert into a place of abundance (Mt 14:13-19).

The Renunciation of Possessions

As we have seen, persons from the affluent classes were also part of the community of Matthew. Placing oneself under the new sovereignty of God over Israel imposed, however, very concrete obligations. Fulfilling the law of Moses was no longer sufficient (Mt 19:17-20); rather one had to accomplish the renewed justice of the messianic community, as proclaimed by Jesus in the Sermon on the Mount. There Jesus explicitly called for detachment from material riches to have riches in heaven (Mt 6:19-21). Detachment is also asked of the rich young man who wanted to follow Jesus: "Sell your possessions and give to the poor, and you will have treasure in heaven. Then come, follow me" (Mt 19:21). Entering the messianic community under the sovereignty of God requires a renunciation of possessions, and for the rich that means a separation from their riches. It is interesting to observe that, while the Gospel of Mark indicates how difficult it is for "those who have possessions" to enter into the reign of God (Mk 10:23),

Matthew simply speaks of how difficult that is for "the rich" (Mt 19:23). This difference probably reflects the different social situation of the community of Matthew, which had relations with more affluent persons than did the groups to whom Mark's Gospel was directed.[23] Nonetheless, the same was asked of these persons as of all the other members of the community: the renunciation of possessions (Mt 19:27).

It is important to note that Jesus is not recommending a simple ascetic exercise of detachment, but is rather stating the conditions for entering into a new community. In order to enter into new bonds of solidarity, one has to become free of the economic, social and familial bonds in which were found the old securities. To be sure, these new social bonds seek to be effective and to truly overcome poverty. In fact, those who leave their own house, brothers, sisters, father, mother, children or properties are promised a hundred times more, and eternal life besides (Mt 19:29).[24] It is not a question of vague promises. In fact, historical research shows that the communities of Matthew and John, both possibly situated in Palestinian territory, found themselves in a better economic situation than the first group of Jesus' followers and also than the first community in Jerusalem.[25] We do not know concretely how far the solidarity among the members of Matthew's community extended, or what concrete economic forms the community adopted.[26] Nor do we know to what extent the rich lost not only their possessions but also their social standing, due to the ostracism of a society that rejected the Christian group. This phenomenon was possibly greater in John's community than in Matthew's (Jn 12:42). What we do know is the sense in which Matthew understands the good news for the poor: it is the good news of the beginning of a new community, over which God exercises his reign and which already does away with the poverty of present history.

Obviously, detachment from private wealth, together with solidarity among all the members of the community, can make both wealth and poverty disappear in the community, at least in their more extreme forms, but will not necessarily do away with differences of power and prestige within the community. Thus we understand the importance in Matthew's Gospel of Jesus' sermon on life in community (Mt 18:1-35). In this sermon not only are we reminded that the most important in the reign of God are those who humble themselves and become like a child or a servant (*paîs,* Mt 18:4); not only are we warned against the possibility of despising the "little ones" of the community (Mt 18,10), but we are also told that the ultimate decision about internal problems belongs to the community as a whole (Mt 18:15-22), and we are given very concrete instructions about the manner in which reconciliation is to be reached (Mt 18:15-35). Matthew is worried about the possibility that in the messianic community, renewed by Jesus, there will again appear social differences, even if these are simply differences of power and prestige (Mt 20:25-28). He therefore warns against using titles such as "teacher," "guide" or "father." The messianic community is a society in which all the members are brothers and sisters, so that only God is Father and only Christ is guide (Mt 23:8-10).

In this way the beatitudes take on a very concrete meaning. If we were to take them as referring to all poor people, they would be difficult to understand, because by no means do we see in history that those who suffer are consoled, that the humiliated inherit land, or that those who hunger and thirst for justice are satisfied. The easy temptation then is to spiritualize the beatitudes and convert them into a message about the great beyond. But the message of Jesus refers to real poor people. Again, certainly not all poor people are consoled or inherit land, nor are their demands for justice satisfied. What we see in our day-to-day history is quite the contrary: the poor are humiliated, dispossessed of their lands and deprived of all justice. It would be an insult to proclaim these people "blessed."[27] Nevertheless, there are some very concrete poor persons who can indeed be called "blessed" in a very concrete historical sense, free of all spiritualist mystification. They are the poor people who enter to become part of the messianic community. They place themselves under the sovereignty of the reign of God (Mt 5:3), they are consoled (Mt 5:4), they inherit the promised land (Mt 5:5) and their longings for justice are satisfied (Mt 5:6). To them are united the compassionate, those of pure heart and those who work for peace, thus forming themselves into a new society of brothers and sisters, in which poverty, injustice, violence and oppression all disappear. The beatitudes can indeed be seen, and those who see them are blessed (Mt 13:16).

The Universal Perspective

One might think that we are dealing here with some type of isolationism or sectarianism, which holds that the only important thing is the betterment of the situation of a few people. This, however, is not what the biblical text is saying. The biblical perspective takes into account the fate of *all* poor people. But the liberation of the poor, since it is historical, necessarily takes on a particular, concrete form. This liberation is a dynamic that has been inserted into the history of salvation, starting from the election of a quite particular nomad, Abraham, in order to bless, from his group, all the families of the earth (Gen 12:3). The overcoming of poverty necessarily begins in a concrete place at a specific historical time. And this place is precisely the messianic community of the renewed Israel. This community does not remain isolated, but has a universal mission. It is especially called to be the salt of the earth and the light of the world (Mt 5:13-16), manifesting to all humanity a viable alternative. In the Hebrew scriptures, this alternative was destined to become, in the messianic times, a center of worldwide attraction to which all the peoples of the earth would make pilgrimage, coming to form part of the community of Israel (Is 2:2-5, etc.). In the Gospel of Matthew this perspective is in a certain way inverted: it is rather the disciples who disperse themselves through all the earth, making disciples of all nations (Mt 28:19-20).

In the course of history, the messianic community persists as a community that does not identify itself with society as a whole, but represents an alternative to society. It does not impose the new justice on anyone, nor does it use violence to achieve a different society. The only way to create this alternative society is through people entering it of their own free choice (Mt 19:22). Nevertheless, the messianic community does not remain indifferent to the fate of the poor who are not part of the community. The recipients of the possessions that the disciples renounce are the poor in general (Mt 19:21), and not the members of the Christian community, who possibly no longer live in extreme poverty (*ptokhós*). Moreover, the fraternal community not only worries about its own members, as do the pagans, but also is open to those who are not brothers or sisters (Mt 5:47). Most importantly, there are now, against the universal backdrop of poverty, some people who are "poor in the Spirit," who represent the alternative of a new form of society.

Now we can understand concretely the meaning of the expression in Matthew 5:3: "blessed are the poor *tô pneúmati.*" It is not a matter just of spiritual poverty, such as simple interior detachment from wealth, which leaves everything external the same. Neither is it a matter of "poor with spirit," in the sense of the more courageous and organized poor; nor of the "poor in spirit" of Qumran (1QM 14,3.7), in the sense of a forced marginalization because of rejection by official Judaism. Moreover, it concerns something more than the *anawim* who hoped for all from God (Ps 40:18). We are dealing here with poor people who not only hope for all from God, but who already receive from God the consolation, the promised land and the satisfaction of their longings for justice. They are the poor who "with the Spirit" have received from God a new community in which poverty and oppression disappear. It is a community that is made possible precisely by the Spirit who through Jesus, has been handed over to all his followers (Mt 3:11; 10:20). For that reason they are going to cease to be poor, at least in the most extreme meaning of the expression (*ptokhós*). But they continue to be "little ones" (Mt 10:42; 11:11; 13:32; 18:6, 10-14), and "simple folk" (Mt 11:25; 21:16), because they represent before humanity that which God wishes to do with all the poor of the earth. They can therefore easily become the object of the wrath of the most powerful and targets of persecution.

In any case, the poor possess, in the Gospel of Matthew, a hope. It is the same hope promised them by all of primitive Christianity: the beginning of the reign of God already on this earth. This reign of God is not exercised principally in the clouds or in souls, but over a concrete people in history, the people made of those who have Christ as king (Mt 25:34-40). God's coming close, in Christ, to reign means that God will exercise sovereignty over his people, renewing them and separating them from evil guides, who bring them to disaster (Ez 34). For that very reason, the reign of God is good news for the poor. The reign of God means the end of poverty and oppression. The hope of the poor, in this perspective, is not directed toward what some "benefactors" can do for them. The hope of the poor is that God, from below and starting now, has initiated in the history of humanity a different society, in which hunger and thirst for justice are satisfied, in which lands and properties are shared, and in which all sufferings are consoled. The persecutions and hardships which continue to be experienced in history do not negate that fundamental good news: the poor in the Spirit receive the reign of God, because they constitute a people over whom God himself rules.

HOPE IN MATTHEW 25:31-46

Having arrived at this point, we can now try to understand, from a broader perspective, the possible meaning of the final judgment scene[28] and how it can articulate concrete hopes for the poor of this world.

The Ones Who Are Judged

The Nations in the Final Hour

According to Matthew's text, those who are judged are "the nations" (Mt 25:32). In Matthew's language, the term "nations" (*éthnos*) *always* refers to non-believing peoples, as opposed to the people of Israel. Even the designation "Galilee of the Gentiles" (Mt 4:15) probably alludes to its geographic location (Is 8:23-9:1), to the role it played in the history of the northern kingdom and to the influence of paganism in that region. The handing over of the reign of God to an *éthnos* different from Israel (Mt 21:43) is done precisely in contraposition to Israel. The judgment scene in Mt 25 refers to the crisis of Israel as God's people, and to the entrance of the former Gentiles into the new people of God. Other texts in the Gospel of Matthew leave no doubt in this regard: the "nations" are the non-believing peoples.[29]

The literary context in which the evangelist places the judgment scene also suggests the interpretation we are offering here. The scene of the judgment of the nations appears after a series of exhortations and parables in which Matthew describes the attitude that members of the messianic community of the renewed

Israel are to have as they await the second coming of the Messiah (Mt 24:32-25:30). The believers are described as slaves (*doûlos*) who await the arrival of their Lord (Mt 24:45-50; 25:14-30), or as maidens who, as in an oriental harem, await the arrival of the bridegroom (Mt 25:1-13). The social resonances are quite different from those suggested by the "nations" judged in Matthew 25:31-46. The maidens and the slaves are persons in a situation of dependency, and the "social" exhortation is directed primarily at better treatment of their own companions in slavery (*syndoûlos*). If these parables in some way reflect the social background of the members of Matthew's community, then the contrast with the economic and social capabilities of the members of the "nations" is remarkable. If what is at stake in these parables is not past social origins, but the new situation of those who have no other master than Christ (Gal 1:10), then it is quite clear that these slaves know perfectly well who is the Lord for whom they are waiting and they recognize him when he arrives, as opposed to what happens with the members of the "nations," who know nothing about Christ and his message (Mt 25:37-44).

The Believers in the Final Hour

In reality, the Gospel of Matthew has foreseen a different situation for the members of the messianic community in the final moment of history, as Jesus proclaims: "Truly I say to you, in the new world, when the Son of Man shall sit on his glorious throne, you who have followed me will also sit on twelve thrones, judging the twelve tribes of Israel" (Mt 19:28). The members of the messianic community are seated beside Jesus in the judgment. This is the judgment of Israel, over whom hangs its rejection of the Messiah. The norm for judging the twelve tribes is none other than the messianic community itself, in which the most authentic heritage of Israel has been renewed. Properly speaking, however, the messianic community is not judged, either in the judgment of Israel or in the judgment of the nations. All that is asked of the messianic community is that it maintain itself as the true community of the Messiah. That is, that it not cease to await the return of its Lord (Mt 25:5), that it carefully administer the resources which the Lord has entrusted to it (Mt 25:26-27), and that it not allow to appear in the bosom of the community behaviors that are inappropriate for the new society (Mt 24:49).

It is interesting to note the difference between the fate of the condemned in Matthew 25:41-46 and the fate of those members of the messianic community who do not correctly await the arrival of their Lord. The members of the "nations" who have not given food to the hungry, drink to the thirsty or lodging to the pilgrim are thrown "into the eternal fire prepared for the devil and his angels" (Mt 25:41-46). In contrast, the maidens who have stopped waiting for their bridegroom simply remain outside the nuptial chamber (Mt 25:11-12), and the servants who have not carefully administered the resources which the Lord has given them are thrown into the outer darkness, where there will be weeping and gnashing of teeth (Mt 25:30). In the case of the servant placed in charge of the household, we are also told that he will participate in the fate of the "hypocrites" (Mt 24:51). This may suggest an association with the fate of the false guides of Israel, who are always designated by this term,[30] since at root their sin is the same. Both the wicked servant and the false guides, through their desire for power, have converted what was to be an alternative community into a society like any other, characterized by inhumanity and domination.

Nonetheless, in none of these latter cases is it a matter precisely of an eternal punishment (Mt 25:46), but rather of an expulsion. The image used is that of remaining outside a nuptial feast, or that of being thrown out of a bright place. In fact, we are dealing with the same discipline that Matthew has foreseen for the Christian community. When a member does not hear the reprimands of other companions, nor the reprimands of the community of companions as a whole, the member simply comes to be considered as a pagan or a publican, that is, as a person who does not form part of the messianic community (Mt 18:17). In this sense, God's discipline is identified with the discipline of the community itself (Mt 18:18). This expulsion from the community, however, does not mean an eternal punishment. When the young man who wanted to follow Jesus asks him what he must do to attain eternal life, Jesus answers him with a synthesis of the Mosaic commandments: do not kill, do not commit adultery, do not steal, do not give false testimony, honor your parents, and love your neighbor as yourself

(Mt 19:18; cf. 7:12). In no instance is it said that belonging to the community of the Messiah is a condition for gaining eternal life. To refuse to follow Jesus is to renounce fullness or perfection, but not necessarily salvation (Mt 19:21).

The destiny of the members of the messianic community is, therefore, clear. They will enter to celebrate the wedding feast with the bridegroom when he comes. The text takes for granted that the members of the messianic community are concerned for the poor: they are precisely the ones who have renounced all their possessions in benefit of the poor. But not all form part of that community. There are Jews who have not followed the Messiah, perhaps because of attachment to their riches.[31] There are also those false members of the community who will be expelled from it by the Lord upon his arrival. And finally there are all the pagan peoples. It is with these, not with Christians, that Matthew 25:31-46 is concerned. Those who do not belong to the messianic community will be judged according to their attitude toward "the least brethren" of Jesus (Mt 25:40). Who then are these least brethren?

The Least Brethren of Jesus

The Least Brethren Are the Messianic Community

Let us begin by analyzing the crucial passage in which Jesus states: "Truly, I say to you, as you did it to one of the least of these my brethren (*henì toùton tôn adelphôn mou tôn elakhístōn*), you did it to me" (Mt 25:40). What exactly do these words mean?

The word "brother" (*adelphós*) or "sister" has two possible meanings in Matthew. On the one hand, the term can allude simply to the family relationship of persons with the same ancestry.[32] On the other, the term "brother" is used, just as in the Old Testament, to designate members of the people of God, in which new fraternal relations have been established.[33] The members of the messianic community have broken their family ties and have come to form part of a new fraternity, in which all are brothers and sisters, sons and daughters of one Father.

It is very important to observe that, in this fraternal community, Jesus himself designates the rest of the disciples as "my brothers" (*toîs adelphoîs mou*, Mt 28:10), as much as he also may be the "guide" of them all (Mt 23:10). When they tell Jesus of the presence of his mother and his brothers, he extends his hand "toward his disciples" and says: "Here are my mother and my brothers" (Mt 12:49). The characterization of those who fulfill the will of the Father as brothers of Jesus (Mt 12:50) does not in principle propose to extend the same fraternity to all people who live ethically in any part of the world. Rather it contrasts the situation of the community of the disciples of Jesus with a society that has not fulfilled the will of God, despite its rhetorical claims to have done so (Mt 7:21). The community of Jesus, in which there are even prostitutes and publicans, has fulfilled the will of God, while the rest of Israel has not (Mt 21:31). Indeed, the "will of God," in Matthew's language, means precisely the divine plan of salvation (Mt 6:10; 26:42), and not simply the fulfillment of general ethical norms. In this divine plan of salvation, an essential role is played by the messianic community in which a new humanity is beginning, one free of injustice and domination. Precisely for that reason, the "will of God" appears expressly linked to the charge that not one of the "least" members of the community should be lost (Mt 18:14).

The designation of these brothers as "the least" or "the most insignificant" (*elákhistos*) points basically in the same direction. The Gospel of Matthew begins by stating that Bethlehem, "by no means the least among the rulers of Judah" (Mt 2:6), will be precisely the setting in which salvation begins. Indeed, the reign of God begins as "the littlest" (*mikróteron*)[34] of seeds (Mt 13:32). For this reason it is not strange that Matthew uses the term "little" (*míkros*) to designate the disciples of Jesus (Mt 10:42). In this case, his use of the term is a designation for the disciples as such, and not simply for a part of the community of disciples. It is true that in the sermon on life in community, Matthew uses the term "little" several times to designate the weakest sector of the community (Mt 18:6,10,14), and not the community as a whole. He also uses the term "little," with a similar meaning, in order to state that the littlest in the reign of God is greater than John the Baptist (Mt 11:11). In all these cases, Matthew uses material common to the synoptics, which can serve as a warning about the establishment of differences of status among the disciples.

In fact, Luke also perceives the community of Jesus as a little group, a "little flock" (Lk 12:32). Nonetheless, what is quite characteristic of Matthew is the perception of all the disciples as "little ones," those by whom, despite their littleness, all those who do not belong to the messianic community will be judged. Matthew explicitly tells us so, well before the judgment scene: "He who receives you receives me, and he who receives me receives him who sent me . . . Whoever gives to one of these little ones even a cup of cold water because he is a disciple, truly, I say to you, he shall not lose his reward" (Mt 10:40-42). The subject here is not the weakest in the community; rather it is a discourse that at the beginning is directed at the twelve, and progressively becomes extended to the whole community (Mt 10:26-39). In this way, the community of "these little ones" is converted in the Gospel of Matthew into a criterion for judging those who do not belong to it. This is perfectly coherent with what Jesus states in the final judgment: "As you did to one of the least of these my brethren, you did it to me" (Mt 25:40).[35]

Thus is it finally understood why the little ones are designated as "these." Those who have left all and followed Jesus are not absent from the judgment, but are present at it (Mt 19:28). It is a crucial presence, because the messianic community constitutes a norm by which the pagan nations will be judged. As we will see in what follows, however, the messianic community is not the only criterion.

The Least Brethren Are Not the Messianic Community Alone

The actions for which the pagans in the judgment story are called "just" (Mt 25:37) involve attending to the needs of the "most insignificant brothers" of Jesus. It is interesting to note that, although Matthew's terminology seems to refer above all to the treatment of members of the messianic community, the actions of the pagans do not seem to be governed by that same criterion. The pagans, as we have seen, know nothing at all about Jesus' message, and even seem to be ignorant of the existence of the messianic community. At least, when they attend to the hungry, the thirsty, the naked and those who are strangers and imprisoned, they don't seem to do so because these persons are disciples of Jesus. In contrast with what happens with the glass of water which is given to certain persons only because they are disciples of Jesus (*mónon eis ónoma mathetoû*, Mt 10:42), the pagans in the judgment story seem to be unaware that those whom they serve are disciples of Jesus. The motivation for the pagans' just works *seems to be simply compassion before the suffering of others*, and not any consideration of whether the persons in need are or are not disciples of Jesus.[36]

This interpretation could be suggested at two points in the text. First, when there is mention of "one of the least of these my brethren," the Greek term for "one" (*henî*) does not indicate numerical unity, but has, as in Spanish, the meaning of "any one."[37] As we have said, the other terms ("my brethren" and "least") point more clearly to members of the community of Jesus. It is interesting to observe, however, that when it comes to the "wicked" (Mt 25:41), who have not had compassion on the needy, Jesus no longer refers to the latter as "my least brethren" (Mt 25:40), but simply as "the least." Literally Jesus says: "As you did it not to (any) one of the least of these, you did it not to me" (Mt 25:45). There would seem to be in the text, then, a tendency toward universalizing the terminology that at first refers to the members of the community of Jesus.

This universalization is not coherent with certain statements contained in the Gospel of Matthew. For example, in the middle of the Sermon on the Mount, Jesus sums up the Torah of Israel in the following way: "Whatever you wish that others would do to you, do so to them; for this is the law and the prophets" (Mt 7:12). Similar formulations are found in the most diverse religious traditions of humankind, including the Udanavarga of Buddhism, the Mahabharata of Hinduism and the Confucian Analects. They also appear in the deuterocanonical books of the Old Testament (Tob 4:15) and in the Talmud. Jesus possibly gives a more positive meaning to this maxim when he not only prohibits doing to others what we do not want done to us, but also exhorts us to do for them what we would want done for us. We already saw that when the rich young man asks Jesus what he must do in order to attain eternal life, the answer contains a summary of some fundamental ethical precepts of the law (Mt 19:18-19). Certainly, this summary includes something of the characteristic elements of Judaism, such as loving one's neighbor as oneself. Nevertheless, in both cases we are dealing with teachings that in large part would be available to a philosophical ethics independently of revelation. Ultimately it is a question of actions that adopt the perspective of the other, putting oneself in the other's place and leaving aside one's own interests and categories.[38]

And this is precisely what the pagans do when they enter into solidarity with the needy. They are not being judged for their attitude toward a community whose importance they do not know, but for their attitude toward all the little and insignificant people of the world, whether they are believers or not. Still, it is important to observe that these persons are not being judged according to a catalogue of ethical norms. The ultimate criterion of the judgment is their attitude toward Jesus, even though this criterion has remained hidden from the pagans until the end of time. When the pagans helped the needy, they did not seek to justify themselves by fulfilling ethical precepts; they simply helped people without expecting a reward in exchange (Mt 5:46; Lk 14:12). From the viewpoint of the Christian faith, Jesus suffers on the cross the fate of all the poor, the sick and the marginalized, those apparently rejected by God (Mt 27:46). The identification of God with Jesus Christ therefore signifies not only the offer of pardon for all sinners, but also God's solidarity with all those who are apparently abandoned by God in history. Precisely for that reason, the disinterested encounter with the poor is an encounter with Christ himself. In this way the pagans can be called "just" (Mt 25:37-40), a term normally used by Matthew to designate believers[39] or Jesus himself (Mt 27:19). Having found Jesus among the poor, the pagans are placed, just like the messianic community, under the sovereignty of the reign of God, which also belongs to them (Mt 25:34).

This encounter with Christ in the poor does not imply, however, an identity between Christ and the poor such as would allow the gospel to be reduced to an ethics of charity toward the needy; as Christ himself states, "you always have the poor with you, but you will not always have me" (Mt 26:11). In Christ, there is something more important at stake than simple fulfillment of ethical precepts. In Christ, humanity receives the possibility of being liberated from the vain pretension of self-justification, and thus the ultimate root of all poverty and all domination is destroyed. Poverty, in the gospel, is not idealized or mystified. It continues to be an inhuman condition, not desired by God, which now begins to be overcome in the community of disciples. This community, how-ever, is not the result of human efforts, but a new creation made possible by God through faith. For that very reason, the decisive factor, both for pagans and for Christians, is the encounter with Christ. The Christians encounter Christ when they leave every-thing to follow him in the community of disciples and to await him diligently in the course of history. The pagans encounter Christ in their solidarity with all those with whom God himself, through Christ, has entered into solidarity. Christ is the universal criterion of salvation, both for Christians and for the nations.

Nevertheless, Christ is not found among the clouds. He is found in the community of the brothers and sisters of Jesus, and he is found also among the most insignificant, even when they do not belong to this community. *It is not a question of two distinct me-diations, different from one another.* As we saw above, the messi-anic community represents in history that which God desires to do with all humanity in the face of poverty and oppression: God desires the formation of a fraternal people over whom God can exercise his reign of justice and peace. For just that reason, there is continuity between all the poor of the earth and the messianic community of the disciples of Jesus. In this community, the soli-darity of God with all the poor is made visible for all people. *Pre-cisely because there exists a community of the brothers and sisters of Jesus, among whom poverty and oppression are already being overcome, it is possible to proclaim to all the nations that Jesus has become a brother of all the little ones and desires to do away with their affliction.* A solidarity of God with the poor which does not translate into an already visible overcoming of poverty would leave us on a cross without resurrection; we would not have es-caped the realm of utopias and good intentions. The proof that the Messiah has risen and now exercises the authority of the reign of God consists precisely in the fact that the fraternity that he began in Galilee has now become a project of transformation valid for all the nations (Mt 28:16-20).

The Hope of the Poor

As I understand it, this interpretation of Matthew 25:31-46 is not only more faithful to the biblical text, but is also capable of offering more hope to the poor. Without a doubt, the text tells us of Christ's solidarity with all the poor, to whom he has become a brother by assuming their fate through his life and his death. In this sense, our interpretation can announce to the poor, along with "humanist Constantinianism," Jesus' solidarity with them. Our interpretation, however, can add something essential, which is that the fraternity of Jesus with all the little ones of the earth is not something merely invisible, intentional or metaphysical. Neither is it a fraternity which is made visible primarily in the solidarity of certain people who make a commitment to the poor. All such understandings would do no more than legitimize new forms of domination. The fraternity of Jesus with the poor is not invisible. The place where that fraternity becomes visible is in the messianic community of Jesus' brothers and sisters, for it is precisely there, the overcoming of injustice and oppression has effectively begun. And this fraternity can indeed provide the poor with a very concrete hope: the hope for a world without poverty or domination.

This hope is directed to all the poor, including those who are not believers. They are already able to see in the present a new form of human organization in which there is no oppression or poverty. Faith makes a difference, however, because faith is not a purely interior process, but rather implies a radical transformation of human praxis, including incorporation into a new network of social relations. These social relations are not governed by self-justification, mutual utilization, competition, violence or vengeance, but rather by confidence, equality, peace and pardon. From the biblical viewpoint, such relations are possible only by means of God's intervention in history. This is, however, an intervention that, through the Spirit, is open to all, and that takes place wherever two or three come together to live as brothers and sisters of Jesus. Only then is the overcoming of poverty something more than a cooperative strategy of social transformation, destined to distance itself steadily from the poor. The work of the Spirit is what allows the new community of the siblings of Jesus to remain permanently open to the poor and to continue to be good news and a concrete possibility for them.

From this perspective, the text on which we have commented gives us an additional source of hope. In this text, Christ appears as a glorious king who sits upon his throne to judge the nations

(Mt 25:31-46). In the Gospel of Matthew, God has been present as the great king, seated upon a throne (Mt 5:34-35), whose reign over his people is being re-established. Jesus is explicitly presented on occasions as a king (Mt 2:2; 21:5). His reign, however, will be impugned by the powerful of this world, and during his passion, Jesus' royal title will become a motive for mockery and derision both by the Romans, that is, the nations (Mt 27:29,37), and also by the Jewish leaders (Mt 27:42). The scene of the final judgment, by contrast, presents us with a glorious king who judges over the nations. From the viewpoint of the community of the little brothers and sisters of Jesus, this text is no doubt a motive for hope, for what it tells us is that the apparently feeble reign of Jesus, the crucified one, over his little people will finally be converted into a reign over all humanity, now free of poverty and oppression. The other reigns of history, in which domination and inequality prevail, are destined to be overcome and to disappear. In this sense, the messianic community of the little brothers and sisters of Jesus is in reality not the most insignificant of the societies of the world (cf. Mt 2:6), but rather in its smallness it contains the ultimate secret of human history. In this small community, the hope and salvation of the whole of humanity are at stake.

It is important to observe that the reign of Jesus over humanity and over his people is a shared reign. The members of the community appear on twelve thrones, reigning together with Christ (Mt 19:28). Not only that, but the pagans also are admitted, at the end of time, to the reign prepared for them from the foundation of the world (Mt 25:34). Jesus does not keep his reign for himself, but shares it with his disciples and with all the just.[40] The reign of Jesus is a reign of equality and fraternity, in which Jesus himself is a brother and which already makes itself visible in history in the messianic community of his disciples. The hope of the poor is present, therefore, in human history, starting in the present and starting from below. It does not depend on some benefactors who justify themselves by means of the solidarity they exercise with the needy. The gospel announces to the poor the good news that, starting right now, an escape from poverty is possible, as much as this escape might still be threatened by the powerful of this world and therefore subject to persecutions. Despite that, the community of the little brothers and sisters of Jesus knows that in its midst there has already begun, through Christ, the reign of God over all humanity.

CONCLUSION: HUMANISM AND CHRISTIANITY

What Christian faith proposes, therefore, is something more radical than a simple humanism. The humanist proposals of solidarity—the rational ethical obligations that open us up to the perspective of the other and to the other's demands for justice—are integrated into the Christian message. The Sermon on the Mount explicitly includes a positive formulation of the so-called "golden rule": not only does it prohibit doing to others what we do not wish them to do to us, but it also counsels doing to others what we wish them to do to us (Mt 7:12). The disciples of Jesus are called to become "neighbors" to all those in need (Lk 10:36-37), and not only to members of their own community (Mt 5:46-47). This agenda becomes concrete in a set of actions in which Christians can be of the same mind as non-believers, and which range from charity to political activity.

Nonetheless, the gospel ethic opens up more radical perspectives. The believer is invited to do for the poor something more than any humanist ethic proposes: to believe in the words of Jesus, to renounce his or her own possessions and to begin a new form of life in fraternal community with the little brothers and sisters of Jesus. Rich and powerful Christians must decide between measuring themselves by a general ethic accessible to all human beings (and thus being judged finally by the same criterion as the nations) or integrating themselves into a community in which right now, from the very start, equality and fraternity prevail. From the Christian point of view, this latter option is the only one that will truly bring about a profound transformation of the world.

Indeed, the relationship between Christian faith and humanist ethics involves not only integration and transcendence. It is also a critical relationship. Christian ethics detects a possible deficiency in the humanist calls for commitment to the poor. From the Christian viewpoint, humanism does not touch the ultimate root of human evils, which is undeniably the human pretension of self-justification, based ultimately on the lack of faith. For precisely that reason, the humanist solution to the evils of humanity is never, from the Christian viewpoint, sufficiently radical, and thus humanism is permanently threatened by the tendency to reproduce the evils that it criticizes. Old structures of domination are simply replaced by new ones.

Nonetheless, the Christian critique of humanism can be effective and plausible only when Christianity is able to point out, in the reality of history, the existence of communities in which poverty and domination are in fact being overcome. It may be necessary to state that such communities never ceased to appear in the two millennia of Christian history.[41] Still, the Constantinian identification of the church with society as a whole necessarily implied the tendency to assimilate Christian ethics to the general ethics of society. In this context, we should not wonder at the correlation between Christianity and the general values of pagan humanism. The problem, obviously, is not in the coincidence between many Christian aspirations and the aspirations of a given humanism. The problem is in the loss of the radicalism of Christian ethics, which necessarily brings with it the inability of Christianity to demonstrate in history the efficacy and the possibility of another form of life.

The twenty-first century may possibly, from this viewpoint, provide some space for hope. In fact, Constantinianism began to break down, in many parts of the world, only in the course of the twentieth century. This breakdown has doubtless reflected a profound crisis in traditional Christianity. Certain forms by which Christianity, in Constantinian times, expressed its determination to be an alternative community have been severely shaken—such is the case of monasticism and of religious life in general. It is possible, though, that this turbulence is only the counterpart of a great historical opportunity. In our time, being Christian is ceasing to be the product of a cultural or sociological determination and is becoming the conscious adoption, by the grace of God, of a different way of life. That is what is beginning to be expressed in the new ecclesial movements and in the free churches, despite all their ambiguities.

Hope for twenty-first century Christianity would therefore be formulated in this way. During the century that has just ended, Christians have become progressively more conscious of their obligations with respect to the poor. Confronted by the millions of poor people that the current economic system produces, the churches have heard the voice of Christ, who tells us: "You give them something to eat" (Mk 6:37). During these last decades, we Christians, like the disciples, have asked ourselves in what concrete ways we can get bread to feed the multitudes (Mk 6:37). Possibly the twenty-first century will be the time in which we hear the voice of the Lord asking us, directly, how many loaves we have to share. Only thus does there arise, from right now and from below, an alternative society in which the structures of the system are not reproduced, a society in which hope is now a reality.

4

The Proclamation of the Reign of Jesus the Messiah

In contemporary theology, including both the theology of the industrialized world and the "emerging" theologies, there is a growing consciousness of the unity that exists between the pre-Easter Jesus and his message about the imminent beginning of the reign of God.[1] A fortunate legacy of liberation theology is the awareness that this reign of God has very concrete implications for a world threatened by injustice, inequality, political and military violence and ecological disasters.

We must begin by making a few clarifications about the language we use here, because it is different from the customary theological language. First I prefer the expression "pre-Easter Jesus" because, in contrast to other terms such as "historical Jesus" or "earthly Jesus," it makes it clearer that there is only one Jesus, not two, and that Jesus the Messiah (or the Christ) is not simply a projection of our faith, but the same Jesus who walked the earth. The Jesus who fished on Lake Tiberias, the Jesus who hung from the cross and the Jesus who was raised up are one and the same, and this single person is the one that our faith proclaims Messiah and Son of God. Second, the term "reign" translates better than "kingdom" the dynamic character of the *basileía* (*malkut*) of God, without taking away any of its historicity or its space-time setting, as we shall see.

Did the unity between God's reign and Jesus disappear after Easter, as Albert Schweitzer would have it, when it became clear that that reign had not arrived? Or did that reign arrive in fact,

70

taking the form of the Catholic church, Constantine's empire, Hitler's Reich, or the Nicaragua of the Sandinistas? In truth, it is not always clear what that unity between Jesus and the reign of God can mean for us, since we live not only after Easter, but also after many failed attempts to claim that "the reign of God is here" (Lk 17:21).

Let us try to think it through.

TO PROCLAIM JESUS CHRIST IS TO PROCLAIM THE REIGN OF GOD

In theology there is an almost mechanical repetition of the thesis that the proclamation of the reign of God by Jesus was replaced, after Easter, by the proclamation of Jesus as Christ. I believe that this thesis is completely erroneous for many reasons, starting with the obvious fact that the New Testament shows us that the disciples continue announcing the reign of God after Easter.[2] This proclamation was the essential content of their mission: the great Lucan opus culminates precisely when it gives us Paul announcing the gospel in Rome, where he is literally said to be "preaching the reign of God and teaching about the Lord Jesus, the Christ" (Acts 28:31).

But why is the proclamation of Jesus as Christ theologically—and not just exegetically—inseparable from the proclamation of the reign of God? There is first of all an evident reason, which we mentioned at the start: the Jesus in whom we believe today is in no way different from the Jesus who, before Easter, dedicated himself completely to proclaiming, by works and words, the beginning of the reign of God: "Now after John was arrested, Jesus came into Galilee, preaching the gospel of God, and saying 'The time is fulfilled, and the reign of God is at hand; repent, and believe in the gospel' " (Mk 1:14-15). It is not possible to understand the person of Jesus without this fundamental truth of his life, and neither therefore is it possible today to proclaim him otherwise.

Nonetheless, this fundamental truth of his life still does not clarify for us the sense in which his proclamation of the beginning of God's reign is *true* (and not just an unfulfilled promise), and is therefore something that can be continued by us today, after Easter. Thus it is necessary to add a second reason, referring to our present time: the proclamation of Jesus as Christ is inseparable from the proclamation of the reign of God precisely because Jesus' function after Easter consists in introducing and exercising the reign of God in history. Let us examine this more slowly.

Jesus, the Messiah . . .

After Easter, Jesus has been declared Son of God (Rom 1:4) and has received the name that is above every name, the title of Lord (Phil 2:9-11). The consideration of the titles of Jesus has frequently helped theology to reflect on the ontological reality of Jesus, on his divinity. The identification of Jesus with God in such titles as "Son of God" and "Lord," however, not only has an ontological meaning, but also simultaneously speaks to us about Jesus' function in history: "In Christ God was reconciling the world to himself" (2 Cor 5:19).

This is expressed more clearly by other titles such as "King" (Mt 21:5; 25:34; 27:37; etc.) and "Messiah" (Jn 1:41; 4:25). As is known, "Messiah" is translated into Greek as "Christ," and although the term at times functions already in the New Testament as a proper name, its original meaning should not be lost from sight. For the Hellenistic Christian, the word "Christ" would have meant the same thing that the term "Messiah" meant for the Jewish listener: he is the Anointed. The anointing in this case was the designation of someone for the office of king (1 Sam 10:1; 16:13), and the reign of this king, because he was chosen by God for this purpose, is none other than the reign of God. Precisely for that reason, the separation of the proclamation of the Christ, that is, of the Messiah or the Anointed, from the proclamation of the reign of God makes no sense at all. There is not, nor can there be, a Christ without a reign. Only a radical christological dualism between the "historical Jesus" and the "Christ of faith" has presumed to wrest from Jesus Christ his reign.

To proclaim Jesus as the Christ, therefore, is to proclaim him as the Anointed who has begun to exercise God's reign in history. God's reign has now come to be "the reign of his beloved Son" (Col 1:13). Contrary to what is normally stated, the reign of God does not disappear from Christian faith after the death and resurrection of Jesus Christ. Quite the opposite: what Christian faith affirms is that the reign of God proclaimed by Jesus has already begun in our world, and is now being exercised by the Messiah. Jesus is the King who exercises the reign in the name of God the Father. Thus the Letter to the Ephesians can speak in all propriety of the "reign of Christ and of God" (Eph 5:5).

Reigns in History . . .

Sometimes the reign of God is thought of as a celestial reign, in which Jesus has his throne and to which people go after their death. That, however, is not the idea which appears in the New Testament. To begin with, it is well known that the term "heaven" is a pious manner by which the Jews avoided pronouncing the name of God. The "will of heaven" is the "will of God," and the "reign of heaven" is nothing but the "reign of God." The good news is not the existence of a kingdom in heaven, but the fact that God has begun to reign both on earth and in heaven, that the reign of God has begun in history.

Statements such as "my reign is not of this world" (Jn 18:36) do not mean that the reign of Jesus does not take place in history. What they refer to is, first, the provenance of the reign: this reign that breaks into history is the reign of God, and not a reign created by the powers of this world. Second, therefore, such a reign does not obey the logic of this world, especially the logic of violence and counter-violence: "If my reign were of this world, my servants would fight that I not be handed over" (Jn 18:36).

It might be ventured, then, that the reign of God, although it has begun in history, is nevertheless a purely interior and invisible reign, in which Jesus Christ would be reigning only in our hearts. Cited as evidence would be Luke 17:20-21: "The reign of God is not coming with signs to be observed; nor will they say, 'Lo, here it is!' or 'There!' for behold (*idoù*), the reign of God is *entós hymôn*." This *entós hymôn* may be translated "within you," but also, and more properly, "among you" or "in the midst of you." This latter translation reveals something essential, namely, that the reign of God is not something individual, but rather involves a community: the community of the disciples of Jesus.

This community is visible in history. For that very reason the reign of God, exercised by Jesus, does not go unnoticed by the powerful of this world; on the contrary, it produces anxiety in them and even destabilizes them. For example, some Christians of Thessalonica were accused before the authorities in this way: "These men who have turned the world upside down have come here also, and Jason has received them; and they are all acting against the decrees of Caesar, saying that there is another king, Jesus" (Acts 17:6-7). For the Jews of Thessalonica, it was quite clear that 1) the reign of God is still being preached after Easter, 2) that reign is now exercised by Jesus, and 3) that reign becomes real in history, even to the point of threatening the reign of Caesar.

This is not a simple misunderstanding on the part of those Jews. The Christians themselves perceive this opposition between the reign of God, exercised by Jesus, and the political systems prevailing in the world. Paul says simply that it was "the rulers of this world" (in general) who crucified Christ (1 Cor 2:8), and James says the same referring to the rich (Jas 5:1-6). Such passages indicate not just a generalization of something that happened at one moment on Calvary, but also a perception of what is happening today, in history, after Easter.

The matter is so important that it serves even to predict the fundamental contents of the time that remains between the resurrection of Jesus and the end-time. This between-time is marked by the struggle of the powerful of the earth against God and his Anointed (Ps 2:1-2, quoted in Acts 4:25-26). Similarly, the Book of Revelation foresees that the political systems of the future will be opposed to the reign of Jesus. Nevertheless, Christ will overcome them, "for he is Lord of lords and King of kings, and those with him are called and chosen and faithful" (Rev 17:14). All of history tends toward this one event: the definitive installation of the reign of God exercised by the Messiah (Mt 16:28). As Paul states, first has been the resurrection of Christ, then will come the resurrection of those who are of Christ, and "then comes the end, when he delivers the reign to God the Father after destroying every rule and every authority and power" (1 Cor 15:24). In this way the reign of God, entrusted to the risen Jesus during the time that remains of history, will return definitively to the Father, so that God may be all in all (1 Cor 15:28).

Now, if the proclamation of Jesus implies proclamation of the reign, and if this reign is exercised in history, then why did Jesus not accept being proclaimed king of Israel? John's Gospel tells us that after Jesus fed the multitudes, the people were saying, " 'This is indeed the prophet who is to come into the world!' Then Jesus, perceiving that they were about to come and take him by force to make him king, withdrew again to the mountain by himself" (Jn 6:14-15). What kind of reign is this that does not come about politically? To understand this, we must turn our eyes to the history of Israel.

As King of Israel

Luke's Gospel begins by announcing to us that Jesus "will be great, and will be called the Son of the Most High; and the Lord God will give to him the throne of his father David, and he will reign over the house of Jacob forever; and of his kingdom there will be no end" (Lk 1:32-33). What does it mean to be king of the house of Israel, occupying the throne of David?

To understand the fundamental meaning of God's reign over Israel, we must go to a text that is seldom cited, but that sheds light on the fundamental experience of the Hebrew people, the liberation from Egypt. When the Israelites cross the sea and the oppressor army drowns in its waters, Moses intones a triumphal canticle in which are enumerated all the saving actions of the Lord (YHWH) on behalf of his people. The Lord is not only stronger than the Egyptian state, but is also mightier than the princes of Edom, Moab and Canaan. The song ends solemnly with the acclamation: "The Lord will reign forever and ever" (Ex 15:18). Situated in this context, the meaning of the psalm is clear. Once liberated from the oppressive power of Pharaoh, the Israelite people constitutes itself as a fraternal society in which the injustices of Egypt are not to be repeated, so that in this way the people can represent a compelling alternative for all the nations of the earth. And that means concretely that in Israel there will be no pharaohs, but *God himself* will reign over his people.

The reign of God has therefore a very concrete meaning: there are no other kings over Israel. In fact, this was the case for about two centuries: between 1250 and 1030 B.C., Israel was an acephalous society, in contrast to the surrounding political systems, which were centered on a king more or less sacralized and endowed with priestly functions. The pressure of neighboring peoples, however, brought the Israelite people to desire to have a monarchy "like the other nations" (1 Sam 8:5). Israel did not want to be an alternative society. In the face of the people's demand, the Lord tells the prophet-judge Samuel:

> "Hearken to the voice of the people in all that they say to you; for they have not rejected you, but they have rejected me from being king over them. Thus have they behaved toward me from the day I brought them up out of Egypt even to this day, forsaking me and serving other gods . . . Only, you shall solemnly warn them, and show them the ways of the king who will reign over them." (1 Sam 8:7-9)

These "ways" are in effect the establishment of an army and a royal court, with the consequent increase in violence and inequality among the people.

The reign of God is replaced by that of a human king (1 Sam 12:12) so that injustice and idolatry come to have a common root: the desire to be like other peoples, rather than present a distinct alternative. Of course, God continues to guide his people even through its mistaken choices, so much so that the figure of King David will serve to give concrete form to the messianic expectations for the future (2 Sam 7:12-16). Even David's sin with Bathsheba will produce the dynastic lineage from which the Messiah will come (2 Sam 12:24). But the a posteriori legitimization of the monarchy does not forget that the kings of Israel are not seated on their own throne, but "on the throne of the reign of the Lord over Israel" (1 Chron 28:5; 2 Chron 13:8).

Still, the monarchy collapses because of the infidelities of the kings of Israel and Judah; the temple where God's glory resides falls into the hands of heathens. Faced with this situation, the prophets affirm that the ruin of the dynasty and the temple does not mean the end of the reign of God. God continues reigning over the entire universe and over all the peoples (Jer 10:7-10; Zech 14:9). This means, then, that there is a hope that can be directed to the future, when God will reign again over his people Israel: "the Lord of hosts will reign on Mount Zion and in Jerusalem, and before his elders he will manifest his glory" (Is 24:23).

This hope gradually takes on concrete forms: Israel will again be an alternative society capable of attracting other peoples toward itself (Zeph 3:9-10). That means removing from among the people those "proudly exultant ones," who are ultimately responsible for the idolatry and the injustice (Zeph 3:11). What God will leave behind will be "a people humble and lowly. They shall seek refuge in the name of the Lord, those who are left in Israel; they shall do no wrong and utter no lies, nor shall there be found in their mouth a deceitful tongue. For they shall pasture and lie down, and none shall make them afraid" (Zeph 3:12-13). Then will the people be able to burst out in praise, for God will have become Israel's king again: "Sing aloud, O daughter of Zion; shout, O Israel! Rejoice and exult with all your heart, O daughter of Jerusalem! The Lord has taken away the judgments against you, he has cast out your enemies. The King of Israel, the Lord, is in your midst; you shall fear evil no more" (Zeph 3:14-15).

From this perspective, it is God himself who will personally come to take care of his people, instead of the evil shepherds who have taken advantage of them and brought them to ruin. God himself will reclaim his flock and will take charge of giving them pasture and establishing justice (Ez 34:10,15,17). Therefore, what is promised for the future resembles in a certain way the situation prior to the establishment of the monarchy: a people without kings, different from all the other nations. But the promises for the future resemble the pre-monarchical past only in a certain way, because the promises for the house of David do not disappear; now, though, there is talk of a "prince" (*nasî*), and not necessarily a king (Ez 34:24).

These developments involve certain ambiguities with respect to the figure of the Messiah, who at times comes to be represented even by a pagan ruler (Is 45:1). Nonetheless, what predominates is a certain collectivization of the messianic ideal: the messianic role appears now to be performed by the whole people of Israel, and even acquires decidedly pacifist features (Is 42:1-4). What becomes clear, in any case, is that the great world powers with their bestial and inhuman features, have their days numbered, and that the reign of God will definitively prevail (Dan 2:44). Certainly the figure of the "son of man" is decisive for these hopes, because to this "son of man" will be handed over the true reign of

God (Dan 7:13-14). However, sovereignty seems also to belong collectively to the whole people: "The kingdom and the dominion and the greatness of the kingdoms under the whole heaven shall be given to the people of the saints of the Most High; their kingdom shall be an everlasting kingdom, and all dominions shall serve and obey them" (Dan 7:27).

We began this section by asking how it was possible that the Jesus whom the Christian communities proclaimed as anointed king could be the same person who before Easter rejected being enthroned by his followers (Jn 6:15). In order to clarify the understanding that Jesus might have had of the reign of God, we have examined some basic images about that reign in the Old Testament. Those images certainly reveal the possibility that God's reign might be exercised by a king, one anointed by God for that end. Nevertheless, the introduction of a king is viewed critically by the Old Testament, which moreover documents the collapse of that monarchical project. Obviously Jesus did not want to advocate the reintroduction of a monarchy. That does not mean that the reign of God has disappeared from the horizon of Israel's faith; on the contrary, it is proclaimed anew that *God himself* will again rule over his people. Such an affirmation, however, leaves unclear what will be the characteristics proper to God's reign in history, and what will be the function of David's descendent in that reign. To gain more clarity in this regard we will have to consider that descendent more closely.

TO PROCLAIM THE REIGN OF GOD IS
TO PROCLAIM JESUS CHRIST

Just as the "Christ of faith" separated from the reign of God represents a falsification of the Jesus preached by the apostles—since Jesus, far from being a simple projection of faith, is a real Messiah who exercises God's reign in history—in a like manner, the idea of a reign of God separated from Jesus Christ lacks biblical and theological sense. And this is so for at least two reasons. First, because Jesus is the one who makes it possible to *know* what the reign of God is. Second, because Jesus is the one who makes it possible to *enter* the reign of God. Let us examine this more in detail.

Jesus Makes It Possible to Know the Reign of God

If we did not have the testimony of the first communities about Jesus, we could easily confuse the reign of God with either theocracy or political messianism. Theocracy, on the one hand, proclaims God himself to be the true leader of a given state, which would be constituted politically according to laws given by God for all its citizens. Of course, theocracies easily become intolerant toward those who do not share the same faith or those who contravene the presumed will of God. Moreover, the correct interpretation of the divine will requires a corps of specialists, who in actuality direct the destiny of the state: theocracies are in fact hierocracies (from *hiereús*, priest). While theocracy sanctifies a determined political system by declaring it to be a direct application of the divine will, messianism, on the other hand, denounces the faults and injustices of the social system and promises a rapid solution. Everything will change at the moment when the messianic figure or group reaches political power. Political power is the key for bringing about, from above, the social transformations that are considered necessary.

Both theocracy and messianism differ radically from the reign of God that Jesus proclaimed with his works and words. The reign of God is good news for the poor (Mt 11:5), which neither theocracy nor messianism is, at least in the long run. Theocracy and messianism legitimize present or future domination, having occasional recourse to some type of rhetoric about poor people. What Jesus proclaims, on the contrary, is the end of all domination. It is not a matter of some future abolition of poverty, when the correct group reaches power. The reign of God signifies the beginning, *from right now and from below*, of new social relationships. The accounts of the feeding of the multitudes demonstrate this fact. Jesus not only states, before his disciples, that the hunger of the poor has to do directly with their mission (Mk 6:35-37), but also points out that the task of the disciples does not consist in becoming mediators between the economic system and the poor, in the style of a non-governmental charitable organization. The solution of Jesus is more radical, for it requires the disciples to leave behind the "vertical" logic of the system *by sharing what they have*, because in this way there will be enough for all and more than enough (Mk 6:37-44).[3]

Considered thus, the reign of God is a reign that begins already in history and is not some future event. It is not a static attribute of the divinity, but a function that God exercises practically over history. Of course, this means that there is no reign of God if there is no one over whom God reigns. The reign of God, therefore, needs a community. This was the function of Israel in the old covenant and of the Christian communities in the new. Jesus in fact does not pretend to do anything more than to invite Israel once again to constitute itself as the authentic people of God (Mt 23:37-39). The community over which God reigns is obviously a new community, different from the other peoples of the earth, not to be isolated from them, but to represent *for them* a singular and attractive alternative. The community of the disciples of Jesus, to the extent that they are distinct from the world surrounding them, can be salt and light for that world. It is the city set on a mountain which cannot be hidden, but rather is visible to all the nations, and precisely as such fulfills a purpose on behalf of all humanity (Mt 5:13-16).

The community over which God exercises his reign has, then, certain special characteristics which differentiate it from other human communities. First, as we said, there is real sharing, which eliminates both scarcity and social differences. Precisely for that reason, God's reign is not very attractive for the rich (Mk 10:23), although they are not a priori excluded from it (Lk 19:1-10). Economic domination, though, is not the only kind that disappears. The fact that God reigns implies that *no one else reigns*, for in the reign of God every form of power is inverted, including the power of adults over children (Mt 18:1-5). Only those who become as children enter the reign of God. Even differences based on one's own labor disappear in the reign of God: those who have worked the whole day receive exactly the same pay as those who have worked only a few hours (Mt 20:1-16). This disappearance of differences includes the disappearance of all *paternalism* and of all *patriarchy*. Those who leave family and economic ties to become part of the community of Jesus receive "a hundredfold" in everything except . . . fathers (Mk 10:29-30; Mt 23:9). Indeed, when there is true sharing, no one remains in a position of caring for others, but all care for all.

From this viewpoint, it becomes clear that God's reign, as Jesus understands it, does not consist in a political project, since all political forms involve violence and domination. Concretely, this means that God's reign cannot be embodied in a monarchy, such as the one that began with Saul and ended in the year 587 B.C. To the extent that God reigns completely over his people, every other lordship disappears. Thus God's reign is decisively different from any theocracy, hierocracy, or messianism, for these are nothing more than varying configurations of political power.[4] Faced with the absurd petition of those who want a position of power in the reign of God, Jesus responds by pointing out that "those who are supposed to rule over the Gentiles lord it over them, and their great men exercise authority over them. But it shall not be so among you; but whoever would be great among you must be your servant, and whoever would be first among you must be slave of all. For the Son of Man also came not to be served but to serve, and to give his life as a ransom for many" (Mk 10:42-45).

With this last phrase we touch the nucleus of the reign of God, as Jesus understands it and inaugurates it. We say this for two reasons:

1. Every form of domination, whether economic, religious or political, involves some type of violence. The state seeks no more than to monopolize and legitimize the exercise of violence. Over against such efforts, Jesus proposes the radical renunciation of violence (Mt 5:38-48; 26:52). The renunciation of violence is not simply a tactic to attain certain objectives more effectively, but is a reflection of the very attitude of the God who makes the sun to shine upon the wicked and the good (Mt 5:45). The disappearance of violence in the community where God reigns (Mt 5:21-26) shows precisely that the prophetic promises for the messianic era are being fulfilled in history. In the community of the Messiah, swords are converted into plowshares (Is 2:4). Of course, the realization of the messianic promises in a concrete community does not yet signify the redemption of the whole world, where injustice still reigns. Precisely for that reason, the non-violent reign of God is subject to violence by the powerful and by all who feel threatened by the new order of things (Mt 10:34; 11:12).[5]

2. Jesus accepted that the powerful among his own people would unleash their violence upon him, but he also linked entrance into God's reign with allegiance to his person, so that only those who

follow him in the way of non-violent service can enter God's reign (Mk 8:31-9:1). Jesus proposes that the logic of God's reign entails following him in such a way that anyone who does not have his eyes fixed on Jesus, who opens up the way for us, is no longer fit for the reign of God (Lk 9:62). Thus, the motivation for service is nothing other than Jesus' own service. But this places before us the essential question: Why this linking of the reign of God to the person of Jesus? Put another way, would it not be possible to realize the project of the alternative community proposed by Jesus, without any attachment to Jesus himself? This question will be the subject of the following section.

Jesus Makes Entry into God's Reign Possible

The reign of God—the fact that God reigns—means that no one else reigns in his place, and this involves the disappearance of every human form of domination, from that based on wealth (*mamonâs*, Mt 6:24) to religious, intellectual or political domination: "But you are not to be called rabbi, for you have one teacher, and you are all brethren. And call no man your father on earth, for you have one Father, who is in heaven. Neither be called masters, for you have one master, the Christ" (Mt 23:8-10). We must clarify, however, the function of Christ, the Messiah, in this reign. It might be thought that, similarly to what happened in the history of Israel, the throne that belongs to God is now occupied by a human king. The prophet Ezekiel had indeed proclaimed that, given the disaster which were the kings of Israel, God himself would return to reign again. This proclamation in a way relativized the figure of David's descendent, changing him from a king to a prince (Ez 34:20-24). Is this what happens with Jesus?

The Identification of God with the Messiah

The answer is obviously in the negative. Christian faith affirms that Jesus is the definitive king of the new Israel.[6] However, his reign is not a reign like that of the kings of this world. Quite the contrary. According to the prophecy of Zechariah (9:9), the king of Judea appears as "humble and mounted on an ass" (Mt 21:5). The Lion of Judah is a lamb, slaughtered by the powerful of this world (Rev 5:5,12), and the exaltation of Jesus after Easter does not signify in any way the restoration of Israel's political sovereignty (Acts 1:6-8).

From the viewpoint of the new people of God, the reason is clear: the new communities that arise after Easter do not form a state, in which there would continue to be inequalities, but a free people in which social differences disappear (Acts 2:43-47; 4:32-37). But *from the viewpoint of Jesus himself,* he does not become a sovereign, either earthly or heavenly, who is distinct from God but in whom the divine sovereignty is in some way vested. What Christian faith affirms is precisely that God identifies himself with Christ. As Paul says, "In Christ God was reconciling the world to himself" (2 Cor 5:19).[7] With the affirmation of Christ's divinity, something critical is at stake for the very idea of the reign of God. If God identifies himself with the Messiah, then *there is no one else exercising the reign in the name of God,* as happened in the failed experience of the monarchy of Israel. *God himself* is the one who exercises this reign, just as Ezekiel announced. But this exercise of reigning by God himself does not suppose a limiting of the functions of the Messiah, because *God himself is the Messiah.* For that very reason, Jesus not only exercises the reign over his tiny people, but is at the same time the Lord (*Kýrios*) of all the universe, "King of kings and Lord of lords" (1 Tim 6:15). Thus this tiny people, despite all the persecutions, knows itself to be indestructible.

Now the affirmation of Jesus' divinity does not imply, for Christian faith, any lessening of his humanity. God identified himself with a human person of flesh and blood, and this has great importance for the reign of God. It shows us that God's drawing near to his people becomes concrete not only in a novel and attractive way of life (Deut 4:6-8), but also in the extreme abasement of the divinity, even to the point of taking the form of a slave, making himself similar to us and undergoing the most disgraceful of deaths, being hung on a tree, on the cross of rebels and slaves (Phil 2:6-11). The equality that characterizes the reign of God occurs in God himself made man. The service which characterizes the reign of God takes flesh in a God who takes the form of a servant. The non-violence that characterizes the reign of God takes flesh in God himself who becomes obedient unto death, even unto death on the cross. It is a great scandal, not only for the Jewish religion, but for every religion, even those that allow "incarnations," and for every pagan humanism: God personally identifies himself, not with some haughty intellectual, priestly or political figure, but with a crucified victim.

This twofold affirmation of both the divinity and the humanity of Jesus is enormously important for the internal logic of God's reign. If God has identified personally with his Messiah, it is God himself who rules over his people. Hence there is no messianic figure who can govern in God's place, occupying his throne. Every messianism is excluded. The only head of the Christian communities is Christ himself (Eph 1:22), in whom they all have their unity (1 Cor 1:12-13). That means, then, that in the Christian communities there is only one mediator between God and humans: Christ himself (1 Tim 2:5). The former priesthood is superseded, for Christ himself is the only priest necessary (Heb 7:22-25). Moreover, God's rule over his people has just the form that has been revealed in Christ: it is the service of the Lamb, gentle and lowly in heart, whose yoke is easy and whose burden is light (Mt 11:29-30). Any theocratic authoritarianism is meaningless here. God himself has become our first-born brother (Rom 8:29), bringing us into relationship with the only one who can be called *Abba*, Father (Rom 8:15). Precisely for that reason, the Christian community is a community of brothers and sisters, free of all domination (Mt 23:8-9).

Thus we encounter a new and surprising characteristic of God's reign. The identification of God with the Messiah not only makes it possible for God himself to reign over his people. In God's identification with his suffering Servant, the reign of God acquires an unexpected dimension, though it is one with deep roots in the Old Testament (Ex 19:5-6): in the reign of God, the brothers and sisters of Jesus are made with him *into kings and into priests* (1 Pet 2:9; Rev 1:6; 5:10).[8] There is no more effective way of affirming the disappearance of all social differences in God's reign. As Paul says, "There is neither Jew nor Greek, there is neither slave nor free, there is neither male nor female; for you are all one in Christ Jesus" (Gal 3:28). As the book of Daniel has already announced, sovereignty in the reign of God is transferred to all God's people (Dan 7:27), who reign and exercise priestly functions for the good of all humankind. The reign of God's people, however, does not involve any worldly exaltation or power. To the contrary, God's people continues the servant mission of the Lamb. And like the Lamb, Christ's followers also suffer persecution, for the reign and the priesthood of the Christian communities consist in being a visible assembly over which God is already exercising his reign, and the realm, therefore, where all the powers of this world are being cast down.

The Lamb Who Frees from Sin

The preceeding reflections reveal to us the essential meaning of Jesus for the very structure of God's reign. It is precisely the presence of the God who has identified himself with Jesus Christ that makes possible the human equality proper to God's reign (2 Cor 8:14), which Israel could not realize fully. One might still reflect, from an agnostic and humanistic perspective, that all this sounds very interesting, but Christians themselves have never realized it in history. Or, if they have realized it, it has been in minority communities on the fringes of the central currents of Christianity. Humanists believe that the project of an egalitarian community can be realized apart from any reference to Jesus or God. In order to bring about "utopia," they say, it is only necessary to eliminate those economic, social and political obstacles that favor the domination of some human beings by others.

In response to such claims, Christian faith holds that the reign of God is precisely *of God*; it is not of human beings, who therefore cannot bring it about simply according to their desires. All too often, even Christians are heard to say that they are going to "construct" the reign of God. Such a pretension is both naive and completely at odds with the basic meaning of salvation history. If salvation history, as we know it through the scriptures, says anything, it is that God is the source of salvation, and that humanity cannot save itself. When we talk of "structural sin," for example, we had best not forget that, by using such terminology, we are saying precisely that the *structural* evils that humanity faces are not simple moral faults that human beings can correct by themselves, without help from God. When we claim that a *sin* is structural, we are saying that an alternative to it is possible only by the initiative of the one who pardons the sins of the world. And in

Christian faith, that one is none other than the God who has identified himself with Christ.

According to enlightenment humanism, human beings are good
by nature, and the causes of evil are in the society into which we
are born. This is obviously a rather naive schema, which does not
explain satisfactorily how an evil society is possible, if those who
make it up are originally good. In any case, we find in the New
Testament another way of thinking, one that relates the structural
evils of society to the very *structure* of the human heart. As Jesus
says: "From within, out of the heart of man, come evil thoughts,
fornication, theft, murder, adultery, coveting, wickedness, deceit,
licentiousness, envy, slander, pride, foolishness" (Mk 7:21-22). This
obviously does not mean that the human being is incapable of
doing good. Such an extreme theological doctrine has little basis
in the Bible, for even after the sin of Adam, the human capability
to resist sin is affirmed (Gen 4:7; cf. Deut 30:15-20).

The question here is not about the ability or inability to do
good, but about whether one can do good *apart from God*. Jesus
states precisely that no one is good but God (Lk 18:19). The "good
actions" of humans apart from God are at root nothing more than
a strategy of self-justification. This is precisely what Jesus says to
the Pharisees: "You are those who justify yourselves before men,
but God knows your hearts; for what is exalted among men is an
abomination in the sight of God" (Lk 16:15). Doing good no doubt
gives rise to social approval. When human beings fulfill certain
norms, or live up to certain expectations, society applauds and
admires them. However, a good action thus realized lacks all gra-
tuity, seeking rather to gain results or rewards, to affirm one's
own justice before others, or even before God. This is what we are
told, for example, in the parable of the publican and the Pharisee
who go up to the temple to pray (Lk 18:9-14), a parable which for
Luke is aimed at those who "trusted in themselves that they were
righteous and despised others" (Lk 18:9). They "trust in themselves that they are righteous" (*pepoithótas eph' heautoîs hóti eisìn
díkaioi*), and therefore believe themselves worthy of some merit
before God.

The logic of self-justification is, at root, the same logic as that
of recompense. In both cases, a correspondence is expected between one's actions and their results. It is expected that God him-

self will enter into this logic, rewarding good actions and punishing bad ones. Obviously, this logic of self-justification implies a profound legitimization of the whole social order. It is no wonder that Luke tells us that the ones who justify themselves are also greedy persons who mock Jesus' disdain for money (Lk 16:14-15). The legitimization of the social order consists in the ability of the powerful and the successful of this world to interpret their well-being as a result of their own actions, according to the logic of recompense: "I'm well-off because I deserve to be." In the same way, this logic allows the disinherited of this world to be portrayed as culpable for their own misfortunes. Thus the disciples' question about a social outcast: "Who sinned, this man or his parents?" (Jn 9:2).

Of course, this logic of recompense, when it is expressed in explicitly religious terminology, tries to portray God as the one who has brought about or permitted the punishment of the guilty. This logic also has its secular form: the different ideologies, to the extent that they seek to preserve the established order, must portray the unfortunate as deserving of their own situation. The same logic is at work when it is said that evil people are ultimately always punished, or when it is claimed that poverty, sickness or failure are the responsibility of those who suffer them. The poor, the sick, the failures are "losers"; the reasons for their failure must be sought in themselves, in their incapacities and immoralities.

The God whom Jesus portrays, however, does not allow himself to be trapped in this logic. The God of Jesus makes the sun to shine upon the good and upon the wicked, and makes the rain to fall on the just and on sinners (Mt 5:45). Instead of being rewarded according to each one's individual merits, all the workers receive the same at the end of the day (Mt 20:1-16). Not only that, but God rejoices more for one repentant sinner than for the ninety-nine who have no need of repentance (Lk 15:7); thus do we understand the parables of the lost sheep, the lost drachma and the prodigal son (Lk 15:1-32). The one who considers himself just has still not discovered his own sin, while the one who knows he is a sinner has at least discovered his profound need of salvation. As John's First Letter says: "If we say we have no sin, we deceive ourselves, and the truth is not in us. If we confess our sins, he is faithful and just, and will forgive our sins and cleanse us from all unrighteousness. If we say we have not sinned, we make him a liar, and his word is not in us" (1 Jn 1:8-10). From this perspective we can understand the Pauline theology of the law. When Paul tells us that the law, being good, was used by sin (Rom 7:7-24), he is basically telling us the same thing. The commandments can be good in themselves. They can even be given by God as a special grace for his people. Apart from God's grace, however, these commandments are utilized by sin as ways to achieve one's own self-justification. Thus do we have the radical opposition between the justice of God and the justice proper to the person who seeks to justify himself (Rom 10:3).

From this perspective it becomes quite clear why all the attempts to construct the reign of God for oneself are doomed to fail. It is not only because the reign, since it is God's, depends ultimately on the rhythms dictated by God and escaping our control (Mk 4:30-32). The most serious reason is that the pretension of constructing the reign of God for oneself reveals a logic of self-justification. The person who believes that he himself is building the reign of God easily considers himself above other people, and will fall into some type of messianism. For that same reason, his calls for equality will ultimately be rhetorical. At the end he will have to say, as the pigs in *Animal Farm*, that "some are more equal than others." Those who seek to build the reign themselves will ultimately want to be called benefactors, just like all the powerful of the earth (Lk 22:25). They will end up proclaiming only themselves (2 Cor 4:5) and their great deeds in benefit of humanity. In such conditions, the reign of God is replaced by a farce in which the structures of domination that hold sway in the world are once more reinforced.

How then is this logic of self-justification, which is so contrary to God's justice and God's reign, to be broken? From what we have seen here, it is obvious that no individual is able to break such logic. If we as individuals were to free ourselves from that logic of sin, the liberation would be a result of our own actions. We would therefore not have broken with that with which we want to break, which is precisely the pretension of being just with a justice that comes from inside ourselves (Phil 3:9). Salvation must come from without, from another. And certainly salvation comes each time that love enters into people's lives. When we truly love, our commitment to the other person is gratuitous and expects no reward. When we are loved, another person makes us just beyond our own justice. Where does the gratuitousness of love come from? If that gratuitousness were something like an achievement of the human species, we would not have escaped from the logic of self-justification. Individual justification would have been replaced by a collective self-justification. Is there an escape? Who will deliver us from this lethal logic? Christian faith proclaims—and no doubt scandalously—that such an escape is possible only through Jesus Christ. He is the Lamb who takes away the sin of the world (Jn 1:29). But why is this the case?

Raised Up for Our Justification

What is the meaning of the biblical statement that Jesus is the one who can free us from sin? (1 Jn 2:1-2). To understand this, we have to recall all the implications of what we have named the logic of self-justification or the logic of recompense. This logic is not just a way of thinking, but a way of being and of behaving. To the degree that we move within such logic, we seek to achieve our own justice as the result of our actions: we ourselves make ourselves just. We deserve our rewards, as we would also deserve our punishments if we acted badly. This also means, therefore, that the suffering experienced in history can be interpreted as the result of our faults or errors. God, in this perspective, is the one who guarantees a correspondence between our actions and the results they obtain, whether good or bad.

The good news of Jesus tells us, to the contrary, that "in Christ God was reconciling the world to himself" (2 Cor 5:19). This means, then, that God suffered the same fate as Jesus. And that fate was none other than the most humiliating of deaths: crucifixion. By the logic of self-justification Jesus appears as a failure, as someone rejected by God, as one accursed (Gal 3:13). However, Christian faith affirms the contrary: it affirms that in this apparent failure, God himself was reconciling the world to himself. Why "reconciling"? Precisely in response to the logic of self-justification, which sees God as the one who guarantees a correspondence between our good and bad actions and their results: rewards and punishments. But if the one who was supposed to guarantee that very correspondence identified himself with Christ, precisely in his being cursed and abandoned by God, then that logic lacks all validity before God. On the cross of Christ, God himself has nullified the logic of recompense: "He canceled the bond which stood against us with its legal demands; this he set aside, nailing it to the cross" (Col 2:14). In the cross of Christ, God has reconciled us to himself.

Through the cross God has borne the fate of all those apparently rejected by God, entering into solidarity with them. And in the cross God has shown himself to be the one who does not keep count of trespasses (2 Cor 5:19). Thus both victims and executioners receive the possibility of being reconciled with God. Normally, in cultures of Christian influence, the possibility of pardoning and repenting is taken for granted. As daily experience shows us, however, pardon and repentance are not so evident, even in a culture that considers them quite easy. The logic of recompense prevents us from pardoning the guilty, and that same logic encloses us in our sins, preventing true repentance, which is not a simple feeling of guilt, but the discovery that we have been accepted by someone who pardons us. The death and resurrection of Jesus Christ, which reconciles both victims and executioners with God, makes possible the reconciliation of human beings among themselves. This is what is shown in so many parables of Jesus (Mt 18:23-35).

Now it becomes clear why we need Jesus in order to enter into the reign of God. The reign of God is not something that we can simply construct by ourselves. The work of God in Christ was necessary in order for the doors of God's reign to be opened to us. As the Gospel of John says, Christ is the door through which the sheep enter (Jn 10:7). Our entrance through that door is not due to our merit, but is a gift of God, a gift we receive when we trust what was announced to us: the reconciliation that God has brought about in Christ. To the degree that we believe that God justifies the wicked, we are freed from the vanity of seeking to justify ourselves. Thus we escape from the logic of self-justification, and we receive a new justice, which comes from God (Rom 4:5). Precisely for that reason, faith is the key for entrance into the reign of God. To those who confess Christ as Son of God are given the keys that make reconciliation possible, and that allow us to enter into his reign (Mt 16:19; 18:18).

All of this does not spiritualize God's kingdom, but rather makes it practical. The existence of communities founded on the word of Jesus, communities in which pardon and repentance are practical, makes God's reign in history concrete. The Christian churches are precisely the realm where God has already begun the reconciliation of humankind (Eph 2:11-22). This has fundamental importance, because that realm is also where true justice, the justice of God's reign, begins. True equality, in the economic as well as in the political and the religious sense, is possible only when we have escaped from the logic of deserts. Only then is it possible to understand that leadership is a service whose goal should be the sharing of that service among all God's people, so that all reach the unity of faith (Eph 4:11-12). For that very reason, if we wish to inaugurate, starting right now and at the grassroots, a genuine alternative to the worldwide civilization of capital, it is not enough to create cooperatives and seek financing from non-governmental organizations. It is necessary to proclaim the reconciliation brought about by Christ, for it is this reconciliation that makes possible the realization of God's reign in history.

It becomes clear then that it is not we who construct God's reign. Rather, we must receive it like the child who is surprised by an unexpected gift, not like the adult who boasts of his works: "Whoever does not receive the reign of God like a child shall not enter it" (Mk 10:15). What we are to do is not so much "build the kingdom," as *seek* the reign of God. That is, we must seek that God *reign* with the justice proper to God, which is precisely what is meant by the charge, "seek the reign of God and its justice" (Mt 6:33).[9] This does not exclude one's own effort. Quite the contrary; in a capitalist world dominated by the logic of self-justification, our work is more necessary than ever. It will be an effective work, however, only when we understand clearly and proclaim plainly that the reign belongs to God, and that it is God himself who has initiated it in history through the Messiah, the Son of David. Our works will then make manifest that we do not ourselves seek to reign; rather, what we seek is that God himself reign, thereby destroying all injustice, all inequality and all sin: "Preach as you go saying, 'The reign of God is at hand.' Heal the sick, raise the dead, cleanse lepers, cast out demons. You received without paying, give without pay" (Mt 10:7-8). Precisely when the reign of God is proclaimed in this way, with words and works, our efforts will not be superfluous, but rather that by which we become true "fellow workers of God" (1 Cor 3:9).

This supposes a hope for history: hope in a final victory of God's reign, when God wipes away every tear, when there is no longer death, nor mourning, nor pain (Rev 21:4). The guarantee of this hope is the resurrection of Christ. If God truly identified with Jesus of Nazareth, death could not hold him down (Acts 2:24). This is the Christian understanding of the resurrection of Christ: that it is nothing more and nothing less than God's identification with Jesus of Nazareth. And precisely because that identification frees us from the power of sin, we can say that the resurrection of Jesus justifies us (Rom 4:25). That is, the resurrection frees us from our pretensions of self-justification and allows there to appear in history a new form of justice, beyond every logic of deserts. The proclamation of Christ is not the proclamation of a historical figure of the past, his ethical teachings or his moral achievements. The proclamation of Jesus is the proclamation of someone alive. Precisely for that reason, we can hope that God's reign can be realized in human history. The risen Christ is the first fruits of the harvest of the new humanity (1 Cor 15:20-23).

It is important to note that God identified himself with a human being of flesh and blood, and not just with his ideas or with his "soul." For that very reason, the affirmation of the resurrection concerns his whole person. It is not simply a matter of "the cause of Jesus going forward." What faith in the resurrection affirms is the *bodily* resurrection of Jesus (Jn 20:27), because Jesus, as a true human being, is not a soul without a body. It may be that we cannot know, with our earthly categories, what exactly constitutes a resurrected body, or as Paul says, a "spiritual body" (1 Cor 15:44), but nonetheless the bodily resurrection of Jesus is essential for Christian hope. Precisely because the resurrection refers to the *entire Jesus*, and not just to his ideas or his spirit, Christian hope likewise can refer to *this history*, and not another. When we hope for "a new heaven and a new earth" (Rev 21:1), we are not hoping simply for "another world," but for this same world, renewed and transformed eschatologically (Rev 21:5). The reign of God is not a reign on the far side of the grave. It is a reign that begins in this history of ours, here where Jesus reigns over his tiny people. It is a reign that, by the "power of the resurrection" (Phil 3:10), is destined to restore all things (Mt 17:11; Acts 3:21), renewing the entire creation, so that justice may dwell therein (2 Pet 3:13) and God may finally be all in all (1 Cor 15:28).

THE PROCLAMATION OF CHRIST TODAY

Having briefly explored these basic concepts of salvation history, we can now draw some conclusions for our proclamation of Christ in the present time.

1. The proclamation of Jesus the Messiah, if it is a proclamation faithful to his person and his word, is our principal contribution to the transformation of the present-day world. Our world, dominated by the capitalist economic system, is not just one characterized by injustice, inequality and oppression. In capitalism the human pretension of self-justification reaches its supreme expression and most exact quantification, which necessarily takes concrete form in injustice, inequality and oppression. Only the proclamation of Christ is able to break with the innermost logic of human sin and its historical manifestations. Many apparently progressive and radical strategies fail to reach the root of the world's evils, and so miss the key to these problems' solution. The solution is the reign of God, and the key to that reign is nothing other than the confession of Jesus Christ.

2. Not just any proclamation of Christ is a proclamation faithful to his person and his word. The proclamation of Christ is inseparable from the proclamation of God's reign, and the proclamation of God's reign is inseparable from the proclamation of Christ. One might conceive of the "construction of the kingdom" apart from the God who reigns and apart from the Messiah through whom he reigns. But one might conceive also of a transformation of Christ into a simple spiritual principle, apart from his reign as effective in history. The true proclamation of God's reign is a proclamation that issues in concrete deeds (Mt 10:7-8), precisely because God's reign is a reign over a concrete people. And the people over whom God reigns is a people in whom the inequalities and the injustices of this world are not repeated. To proclaim God's reign in the present-day world is to show the world, through the

witness of living communities, that a different society is possible, starting right now and from the grassroots, a society in which the economic, social and political inequalities of our world are not reproduced.

3. The proclamation of Christ is so inseparable from the proclamation of God's reign that in the end the two become identified (Mt 12:28). And this identification is operative in history. Every good Jew knows that it makes no sense to state that the Messiah has come already, if the world has not been transformed.[10] The Christian answer to the problem of the persistence of injustice cannot consist in saying that God is not reigning, or that God will reign only in the future, or that God reigns only in another world. The only coherent Christian answer is that God reigns already over a people among whom injustice, inequality, rancor and violence have disappeared: a people that does not prepare for war, a people that practices pardon, a people that does not return evil for evil. Christian communities are not a simple pastoral or political strategy. When they are true Christian communities, they are the visible proof that the Messiah has already come and that we have already in history the first fruits of his reign (Jas 1:18).

5

The Pentecostal Church of the Poor

From the pioneering works of Christian Lalive D'Épinay on Latin American Pentecostalism, up to our present day, there have been numerous sociological studies that treat this vigorous form of popular religiosity. This study by Richard Shaull and Waldo Cesar, however, breaks new ground by including an extensive theological treatment of the Pentecostal phenomenon. To be sure, an incipient Pentecostal theology already exists, and various Latin American Pentecostal theologians have written occasional reflections on the specific characteristics of their movement. We also have available sociological studies of Pentecostalism that treat certain theological variables creatively and incisively. Even so, the book by Shaull and Cesar pleasantly surprises us by dedicating its whole second part exclusively to theological reflection (by a non-Pentecostal theologian) on the relevance of Pentecostalism for the future of Christianity, especially in Latin America and the so-called third world.

This review will be concerned not with the sociological analysis of the book's first part, carried out dutifully by Waldo Cesar, but only with the second part, written by Richard Shaull, one of the pioneers of liberation theology among Protestants. Shaull, who died in 2002, lived and worked as a Presbyterian missionary in Colombia and Brazil until he had to leave because of political persecution. From his chair in ecumenism at the Princeton Theological Seminary, nonetheless, he remained linked to Latin America

---

Review of Richard Shaull and Waldo Cesar, *Pentecostalism and the Future of the Christian Churches: Promises, Limitations, Challenge* (Grand Rapids: Wm. Eerdmans, 2000). Quotations are taken from the Spanish edition.

and published several interesting works on the relation between liberation theology and the Protestant reformation. His age by no means lessened his willingness and ability to learn new lessons. While other Latin American church leaders, both "conservative" and "progressive," write off the "sects" for their "infantilism" or "emotivity," even while they long for a monolithic, clerical Christianity that belongs to the past, Richard Shaull opted for a different path, one that takes seriously Latin America's popular religious movements. In doing so, he remained faithful to one of the basic axioms of liberation theology, namely, that theology is a reflexive "second act," since the first act is the practice of believers. This fidelity accounts for the originality of Shaull's work.

First of all, it is important to note that Cesar and Shaull are by no means naive regarding the ambiguities of the phenomenon they are studying. In fact, their empirical research has centered on the Universal Church of God's Reign, a church native to Brazil that has often been accused of economic exploitation of its members and that has made public interventions of a very questionable nature. Like other Pentecostal churches, however, the Universal Church has enormous popular appeal, and its language and worship have effectively been adopted by broad sectors of Brazil's most desperately poor.

Shaull maintains that present-day Pentecostal churches constitute what the Christian base communities sought to be three decades ago: a true *church of the poor*. To be sure, in the Pentecostal churches there is not much talk of the preferential option for the poor, in part because all their members *are* poor, but also because among them there are fewer social differences needing to be disguised by discourse about the poor. The fundamental equality of all believers is practiced much more radically in the Pentecostal churches than in the base communities. While such statements may initially alarm the student of classical Latin American theology, Shaull defends his thesis by pointing out that both liberation theology and biblical exegesis have long argued that the poor are in the best position to hear, understand and respond to God's revelation. If this is so, then when the poor become Pentecostal in a decisive way, we are required to be coherent, to rid ourselves of our many prejudices and to remain open to the possibility that the Spirit of God is really active in their midst.

Richard Shaull then asks about the reason for this hermeneutic advantage of the poor. In his view, the marginalized and the impoverished are open to the action of God in history in a way not possible for people who possess security, economic success and power over others. This openness relates quite directly to the Pentecostal experience because, as Waldo Cesar shows in his sociological study, the Pentecostal churches understand the work of the Holy Spirit in a fully material and concrete manner: the power of God is active in daily life, bringing health, material well-being and a new quality of life here and now, to the point that the term "solution" has more weight than the term "salvation." Such an understanding should not scandalize those who have argued in favor of a direct relation between Christian salvation and human liberation. However, the liberation of which the Pentecostals speak does not refer directly to the transformation of political circumstances; rather it has to do with the solution of the immediate problems that poor people face in their everyday existence.

One of Shaull's principal theses is that Pentecostalism is creating a new theological paradigm and changing the traditional conception of redemption in the Protestant world. The new paradigm has three specific aspects: 1) From the Pentecostal viewpoint, the *primary human problem* is not sin and guilt, but poverty, impotence and insignificance, which ultimately are attributable to diabolical forces opposed to God. 2) The *solution* to this problem is not, as in the classical Protestant schema, the gratuitous justification of the sinner, but rather the experience of the risen Christ and his Spirit, which is translated into day-to-day renewal and a guarantee of victory over the diabolical forces. This experience is confirmed concretely in physical healings and sudden improvements in members' well-being. 3) The *human response* called for is no longer faith-as-acceptance-of-forgiveness, but faith-as-boldness to initiate a new interaction with God, daring to ask the impossible and willingness to renounce the little that one has. Obviously, this is the moment that is used by some churches (not all!) to ask their new members for generous donations, to mark the beginning of the concrete changes that will come to their lives. And, as Shaull and Cesar assure us, the changes do in fact occur.

Shaull understands that in this paradigm there is an important coincidence with certain fundamental theses defended by liberation theology, namely, the existence of one single history and the overcoming of the dichotomies between the material and the spiritual. For the Pentecostals, God acts *now*, since Christ has risen and, as someone alive, can do now the very same that he did during his earthly ministry. Poor people do not have to await either the "great beyond" or the arrival of the socialist republic. Redemption therefore becomes something immediate and concrete, something verifiable not only in ecstatic speaking in tongues, but in material transformations that range from bodily cures to obtaining a new job. In all this process, human initiative plays an important role, manifest both in the fervent prayers begging God to come through on his promises and in the boldness needed to break with enslaving bonds and to renounce all one's possessions. In contrast to the classical passivity of reformation theology, the Pentecostals affirm the essential role of praxis transformed by faith. In contrast to the traditional resignation of Catholics, the Pentecostals clearly assert the opposition between God and suffering. The sick are called *not* to accept their sickness; they are invited to "defy" God by asking for a cure. In this way a new Christology and a new ecclesiology come into being. Jesus is a living person who *acts*; he is not a dead man or a static, inanimate formula. The churches, endowed with radically new types of structures and ministries, are the body of Christ, in which the irruption of God's reign into history is made visible.

Shaull, after researching these churches in person and conducting a multitude of interviews, yields to the evidence, but not to the extent of accepting the fundamentalist theology still held today by many (though not all) Pentecostals, or to the extent of becoming a Pentecostal himself. He does yield to the evidence, though, in the sense of recognizing a reality that reveals in an unexpected fashion God's action in history and that therefore requires us to revise many of our old prejudices. Concretely, Shaull believes that "progressive" church sectors have too often accepted uncritically a Western, secularized vision of the world and have even become its proponents. This vision of the world, however, produces only despair among the poor. If theology wishes to learn from the faith of poor people, it must help us perceive and respond to the new manifestations of the Holy Spirit in our midst, instead of hindering a critical analysis of our prejudices. Such a task requires of theologians a recovery of the biblical heritage and a deeper understanding of pneumatology.

In the chapters that follow, Shaull takes some first steps in that direction. Various personal testimonies, not only from Brazil but from Pentecostal churches throughout the world, shed light on the different features of the experience of the Spirit; they show the concrete link between this experience and the world of the poor, and specifically demonstrate its effectiveness in transforming their lives and social relations. Shaull then examines the presence of the Holy Spirit in the resurrection of Jesus, and analyzes the gifts of the Holy Spirit that are present in the lives of believers. Following Raymond Brown, Shaull states that the Holy Spirit is "the presence of Jesus in his absence," and this presence, according to Karl Barth, always means novelty and transformation. Thus the disciples are called to stop thinking about the restoration of the nation of Israel (Shaull applies this to the ideas about struggles for political liberation that we had in earlier decades!) and are invited rather to open themselves to a radical change of perspective and agenda. Responding to such a call does not mean reaching the same conclusions as the Pentecostals, but it does entail a real consideration of their experience, which is the experience of the poor, and of the new possibilities that such experience offers. Only thus will become possible in other churches that which occurs spontaneously among the Pentecostals but which has eluded the base communities: the transmission of a living faith to the next generation.

Thus arise some radical questions about the relevance of the Pentecostal experience to social transformation and about the possible appropriation of such experience by the traditional churches. For Shaull, such appropriation is absolutely necessary, since "any hope for the reconstruction of human life in society today depends above all on initiatives and energies coming from a significant number of poor and marginalized people, through a transformation of their *religious* life." Transformed by an experience of the Spirit, the poor become subjects of their own history, rejecting other dependencies, including clerical ones. Despite the Neo-Pentecostal churches' explicit support at times for parties linked to the status quo, the Pentecostal experience, in Shaull's opinion, includes energies that could well move in another direction—and not infrequently do so. This experience of the Spirit is especially important for the traditional churches, where groups often become active in favor of concrete causes, as happened with liberation theology, but then quickly stagnate, become satisfied with their gains and thus are unable to respond creatively to new situations. In contrast, the Pentecostals possess a "sensational experience of the divine," which creates a state of permanent tension with their world and provides them with an enormous capacity to regenerate themselves creatively.

Citing a thesis of Pentecostal theologian Cheryl Bridges Johns of the Church of God (Tennessee) in her book *Pentecostal Formation: A Pedagogy among the Oppressed,* Shaull states that "Pentecostalism is capable of offering a conscientization process different from Freire's, one that considers seriously the religious experience of the marginalized and thus transforms it into a more effective instrument in the struggle for liberation." Even the simple fact that the Pentecostal churches do not give money to the poor (rather they ask them for it!) signifies a rupture with the attitudes of dependency that are deeply rooted in marginalized people. Citing Cecilia Mariz, Shaull notes that Pentecostalism "makes the poor person cease to be subjectively poor." Such a phenomenon is especially noteworthy among women, who make up the majority in most Pentecostal churches; their spiritual experience produces a new quality of life, with decisive impact on family, church and society. It is not just a question of defined political actions emerging from these experiences; more radically, the Pentecostal experiences can promote a regeneration of life in community from its very bases, since the poor are the primary agents of that reconstruction. In fact, often without even seeking to do so, Pentecostals generate new forms of social organization.

In an epilogue, Shaull calls on the traditional churches to have direct contact with what is happening in Pentecostal circles. He bears personal witness to the ways that such contact has transformed not only his own perception of biblical history, but also his understanding of his task as a theologian, as one who bases his "second-act" reflection on God's unpredictable action in poor people's history.

Shaull and Cesar have been able to draw close to the spiritual experience of the Pentecostals in order to learn from it or, as used to be said in World Council of Churches gatherings, to heed "what

God is doing in the world." This closeness has been developed theologically in a sensitive and suggestive manner and culminates in a quite necessary reflection on the future of Christianity. It is not just that the enormous growth of Pentecostalism in the world (from none in the year 1900 to almost 300 million adherents in the year 2000) is giving a new face to Christianity and to popular religion itself in traditionally Catholic countries. In my view, Shaull's reflection, like that of other authors, is aimed at seeking a continuity with the great intuitions of liberation theology, so that something new can fill the space left empty by that theology. The study of communities in which no one needs to be "the voice of the voiceless" because everyone has a voice (what is the "gift of tongues" if not a charismatic sign of the *linguistic* equality of the faithful?) is, if not a solution, at least a good start.

Certainly, some questions in Shaull's work remain to be answered. A more careful reflection on the ambiguity of religious experience is still needed. I agree with Shaull in his evaluation of the Pentecostal experience as an authentic experience of the Spirit, one that the wise and powerful cannot understand, but that is readily accessible to simple folk. Those of us who have in any way come to know the Pentecostal churches cannot doubt the truth of the experiences that Shaull describes. However, an authentic act of faith can at times, in a second moment, be manipulated or distorted, becoming the opposite of what it originally was. Here I am not referring primarily to the economic manipulations that occur in some churches, but to the ambiguity of the religious experience itself, in which authentic faith can easily coexist with what I have elsewhere called "the schema of the law." In such a case, the original experiences of personal transformation and liberation can easily be changed into a legitimization of the status quo. In this sense, the tendency of Neo-Pentecostals to make politically conservative choices would not by any means be accidental. We should not, however, allow such tendencies to prevent us from defending, sharing and spreading the most authentic nucleus of Pentecostal experience.

Furthermore, serious thought needs to be given to the possible contributions of Pentecostalism to social transformation. Some Pentecostals and Neo-Pentecostals have thrown themselves into politics, at times in rather naive fashion. Shaull appears sometimes to wish that these political ventures were simply more "progressive" in their orientation. Some Pentecostals are, in fact, quite progressive, but the real problem is that Shaull seems to share with the Pentecostals a *Constantinian* understanding of social transformation, that is, a conception of politics in which the principal Christian contributions to social change consist in Christians' participating in and supporting the "correct party" in order to gain political power. Shaull is more radical, and more biblical as well, when he suggests that the truly Christian contribution to social change is in the regeneration, from the bottom up, of all social relationships. To avoid a new Constantinianism, we must keep in mind that such regeneration cannot hope to be realized on the scale of a whole society (except by brute political imposition), but necessarily requires the appearance of free communities in which new social relations are practiced, even if only partially.

What is decisive is how these communities understand their role in relation to society as a whole. Certainly, the simple fact that such communities are endowed with more freedom, participation, mutual aid and fraternity than the rest of society (or the traditional churches) is already in itself a seed of social change. The mere existence of another way of life, despite problems of personalism and abusive leaders, is already a strong reproach, and not a mere verbal one, of a world characterized by poverty, individualism and marginalization. *Often those who contribute most to changing the world are those who least intend to do so.* Nonetheless, a theology that seeks to explain the believing experience of the poor, especially in Latin America, must face this question directly. On this point, the greater part of the Pentecostal world seems to swing between an eschatological, non-political posture (pre-millenarianism) and a right-leaning Constantinianism (post-millenarianism), that is, between traditional Pentecostalism and Neo-Pentecostalism. What needs to be explored seriously is the extent to which the incipient Latin American Pentecostal theology shows signs of a strategy for social change that leaves politicians aside, and sees the vibrant communities arising among the poor as the only gateway to a new society.

Sometimes we find books that we ourselves would like to have written. In any case, this book is recommended reading for those who are seeking new paths toward an authentic liberation of the poor and who are willing to learn from the poor themselves.

6

The Reason for Hope

Reflection on the future of Christianity from the perspective of the new century presents us with an invitation to think about hope, and to do so within a social and cultural context that is not exactly characterized by this "theological virtue." In past decades, many of the great hopes of humanity seemed almost within reach: social justice, democracy, human rights, triumph over disease, etc. The beginning of the twenty-first century finds us in a world in which these hopes seem to have evaporated or to have withdrawn into a distant future. The present period seems to be characterized rather by the sharpening of social inequalities, the persistence of poverty, the global imposition of the capitalist economic system, the continuation of the arms race, the ecological degradation of the planet and other misfortunes. So-called "neoliberalism," as opposed to classical liberalism, no longer thinks that capitalism is capable of overcoming poverty.[1] Such a perception of the economy is completely compatible with all of the "post-modern" ideologies that proclaim those former hopes to be vain illusions, and limit themselves to inviting the shipwreck survivors to a more or less resigned enjoyment of the present—an invitation that on our planet is obviously not extended to all. In contrast, others opt for the "holy folly" of refusing to allow their best hopes to be wrested from them, no matter how deeply into desperation the whole world sinks. Historical folly, however, has the danger of turning into the dogmatic discourse of those who long for a glorious past but are incapable of responding to the challenges of a present in which, when all is said and done, even they have no hope.

It thus becomes important in our epoch to hear again that oft-cited exhortation from the First Letter of Peter, in which Christians are asked to be always ready to respond to those who ask us the reason (*lógos*) for our hope (1 Pet 3:15). This biblical quote has become a kind of slogan for fundamental theology, that is, for the theological activity which asks about the truth of the Christian faith. Nonetheless, the First Letter of Peter is not addressed to a congress of theologians, but to a rather modest Christian community, in which, for example, the exhortation to the slaves to act according to their faith is not accompanied, as in other letters, by a reciprocal exhortation to the masters, possibly because in that community there were no slave owners. It was a community, nonetheless, that had given an original answer to the uprooting and the poverty of its members, providing them a home, reciprocal economic support and a dignified way of life.[2] And possibly for that reason it was a community that had problems with its surroundings. It is precisely when speaking of the possibility of persecution that the exhortation to give reasons for hope appears. The Christians respond to the persecutors, not with evil, but with goodness, with respect and with gentleness. This includes giving reasons for their hope (1 Pet 3:13-17). It is a question, then, of a hope which is not exclusively intellectual, but which has, in some immediate and spontaneous way, a practical character. This is what we must analyze.

THE HOPE THAT IS SEEN

The Enlightenment Vision of Hope

The effort to think of hope in a way that is not purely theoretical, but is rather experiential or practical, would seem to be a common characteristic of contemporary attempts to treat the theme.[3] But what would constitute a purely "theoretical" treatment of hope? The verb *theorein* means primarily "to see" or "to observe." A theoretical approach to hope would seek in some way to make hope seen or observed, so that the contemplation of the world around us would provide us with motives for hope. Of course the reality that surrounds us does not always appear so hopeful. In it we find pain, suffering, oppression. Still, one might think that these realities are only transitory and that authentic reality is, by its own internal dynamism, pointing toward a *future* in which all miseries will be definitively overcome. The great philosophers of the Enlightenment tended in fact to think this way. History for them was a grand process, already visible in the present time, in which humanity would liberate itself progressively both from the yoke of nature and from the yoke imposed by some humans on others.[4]

Certainly these splendid projects of the Enlightenment clashed, even in their own historical moment, with experiences that seemed to give the lie to such grandiose hopes. Immanuel Kant, for example, discovered that the much admired French Revolution ended up devouring its children in the Reign of Terror. Karl Marx was confronted with the failure of the Paris Commune, and Sigmund Freud's dreams of a collective psychoanalysis of humanity came to naught in the horrors of the First World War. Others might mention Joseph Stalin, the Second World War, etc. The reaction of these thinkers to such disappointments was in many cases to try to make hope more *visible*. Since human beings seemed to be incapable of carrying out on their own the emancipatory processes of the Enlightenment, the task of liberation was placed in the hands of other, "macro" subjects. These were to be found in the "laws of history," in "human nature," in "economic laws," in the "Absolute Spirit" or in the "eternal laws of matter"—a series of mechanisms, superior to the human will, which would finally move history along to a happy ending free of misery. The human subjects of history are thus replaced by macro-subjects, destined to carry humanity toward the realization of its deepest aspirations. History, by virtue of its own inner dynamism, would lead humanity, willy-nilly, toward a perfectly reconciled society.[5]

Hope in Liberal Theology

Naturally our present-day culture is suspicious of such optimistic visions of history. Nonetheless, for some time they caused quite a stir, and in some sense it may be said that they fulfilled a positive function with respect to Christianity. Nineteenth-century theology, especially Protestant theology, had to define itself according to the role that Jesus played in the kind of history defined by the

Enlightenment. After a first critical moment, in which doubt was cast on all the supernatural acts which the gospels recount in the life of Jesus, there appeared various attempts to reconstruct the true history of Jesus, apart from faith and myths. Jesus was pictured as a champion of the moral ideals of the Enlightenment. Although today many of these reconstructions arouse little more than literary interest, some of the studies were particularly relevant. In the year 1892, the exegete Johannes Weiss demonstrated something that theology seemed to have forgotten in the course of its history: that the life of Jesus had been completely oriented toward the reign of God, whose irruption into history was considered by Jesus as imminent.[6] Albert Schweitzer, in his famous book on the history of research on the historical Jesus, confirmed and publicized the importance of this discovery.[7] It was, however, a bothersome discovery, since the Jesus who was announcing the immediate coming of the reign of God resembled more a first-century Jew than the moral champion that the Kantian theologians had described.

The possibility still existed, though, of establishing a meeting ground between the Enlightenment ideals and the new discoveries about Jesus. Without a doubt, the reign of God that Jesus preached in the first century involved the disappearance of violence, misery, sickness and oppression, precisely what the Enlightenment had envisioned for the future of humanity. The liberal theologian Adolf von Harnack (1851-1930) had already reduced the message of Jesus to three points: "First, the reign of God and God's coming. Second, God the Father and the infinite value of the human soul. Third, the superior justice and the commandment of love."[8] Nonetheless, it was necessary to show the historical implications of this message, a task that was undertaken by the North American Baptist theologian Walter Rauschenbusch (1861-1918). His theology of the "social gospel" put German liberal theology at the service of the social commitment of believers. On the one hand, Rauschenbusch pointed out the social dimensions of sin, speaking explicitly of "social sin."[9] On the other, he showed the importance of the reign of God in the New Testament, and the eminently social character of that reign. Those who believe in Christ should work for the kingdom of God, which is not a kingdom limited to the human heart, but has to do with the body, with food, with all the social conditions of life. When Christians once again place the kingdom of God in the center of their faith, then the church will cease to be a conservative force, and history's center of gravity will shift from the past to the future.[10] In this way, Christian theology would be able to accommodate the Enlightenment vision of history, which in turn would not be able to hide its Christian roots.[11] The kingdom of God, as a kingdom of peace, justice and fraternity, was the common objective, destined to unite both believers and non-believers in the same historical struggles.

The Reformulation by Pannenberg

The twentieth century was, however, a century of great disillusionment, marked by two world wars, concentration camps, the collapse of Soviet communism, etc. The claim that history, despite everything, contains a promise-filled future becomes more difficult than ever for modern people to believe. Progress ceases to be visible in the present time, and pessimism makes headway. What then is the reaction of Christian theology, once the vision of the future kingdom of God becomes less congruent with the idea of a human race capable of building the reign of God on its own? The German theologian Wolfhart Pannenberg has attempted to respond to this question by claiming that the human race is not the subject, but the "theme" of history.[12] By this he means that the human being is not constituted before history, but rather human identity is constituted in history by means of the processes of receiving, re-elaborating and handing on the diverse traditions. History is therefore not the epic of some human subjects prior to history, nor is it the epic of some macro-subject such as Nature or Spirit. History is the history of traditions.[13] And these traditions are understood by Pannenberg as visions of the world, concurrent among themselves. When a defeated people, such as the ancient Greeks, possess a vision of the world that is more coherent and better able to explain the totality, then the tradition of the conquered ends up victorious over that of the Roman conquerors. Thus, in the course of history, it becomes progressively clearer which is the truest conception of the world, that is, which is the conception that is most coherent internally and most capable of explaining the totality.[14]

Pannenberg thinks that it can be shown that Christianity provides the most complete vision of the totality. This totality is not a purely natural totality; rather, the very meaning of nature is gradually discovered in history. Even the non-believing Enlightenment historian should recognize that it is not possible to understand history without appealing to a vision of the totality, for the understanding of a single historical event requires an understanding of its context, and the understanding of this context requires the understanding of a larger context. Thus any understanding of a historical fact requires ultimately a vision about the totality of history.[15] Now, among many different philosophies and religions, the religion of Israel stands out because it presented a conception of truth as history. For Israel, truth was not the simple correspondence between things and our ideas about them, but was the future fulfilling of promises. The basis of the totality is not simply an account that is limited to explaining the cosmos; rather, the truth of God is tied up with God's historical fidelity to God's promises. Now, Israel lacks a complete vision of history, since the end of history continues to be for Israel a promise. The novelty of Christianity is that it adds to Israel's conception of history an anticipation of the fulfillment of that promise. This is how Pannenberg interprets the resurrection of Jesus Christ: it consists in the anticipation, right in the middle of history, of the end of history. In this way Christianity can present itself as the true religion, since in it appear not only a coherent vision of the totality and a vision of the totality as history, but an already present anticipation of the end of history: Jesus Christ resurrected as the first fruits of the final reign of God. Such a view does not keep the final corroboration of this truth from being incomplete, nor does it prevent history from continuing to be a place of struggle between the truth of God and the power of the evil one.[16]

There is no doubt that these re-elaborations of history, in dialogue with the Enlightenment, have recovered essential elements of Christian hope in the reign of God. On the one hand, emphasis has been given to sin as a social reality; on the other, hope in the reign of God is shown not to be an other-worldly hope, but a hope related to our own history. The dialogue with the Enlightenment has progressed beyond the naive assumption of its idea of history, to Pannenberg's attempt to show that the Christian vision of history is superior to that of the Enlightenment, insofar as it allows a vision of the totality that is impossible without faith in the resurrection of Christ. Pannenberg's proposal, however, is plagued by an important difficulty, one that in a way affects also the Enlightenment conceptions of history. In all these interpretations, hope is founded on the *theoretical* possibility of contemplating the totality of history, and of understanding that the struggles, the conflicts and the miseries of the present time fulfill a function in the totality of history. The starkness of these struggles is alleviated because the vision of history in its totality allows a *meaning* to be found in the happenings of the present, as harsh as they may be. They are the sacrifices necessary so that history may come to a happy conclusion. Now, as Moltmann correctly claims, the result of these tremendous theoretical constructions is that they end up justifying all the evils of history, making them both understandable and necessary in order to reach the earnestly awaited end. God and the evil of the world are thus easily reconciled and harmonized.[17]

In this way, the constrast between a theoretical view of hope and a practical one begins to take shape. The problem is not one of theorizing about hope (that we also will have to do); rather, the problem lies in the fact that these views ground hope in a vision (*theoreîn*) of history in its totality, a vision which evidently is not arbitrary. The Enlightenment would say that already in the present it is possible to see progress in human liberation, while Pannenberg could add that already in the present we have the resurrection of Christ to ground our conception of the totality of history. In either case, we are dealing with a vision of the totality that allows us to understand the present. Nevertheless, when the present is understood from the perspective of a hoped-for totality, whether of God or of a secularized philosophy, the present ends up justified. Of course, such visions of the totality present many difficulties in their philosophical justification. Reality is a radical otherness that can be delimited by our concepts only incompletely and with great difficulty. But there is also an enormous theological difficulty. Indeed, as Paul says, hope that is seen is not hope (Rom 8:24-25). "Theoretical" hope, in the sense of observable hope, is hope that ends up justifying the whole of history, including all its evils, which are seen as the conflicts necessary to arrive at the final triumph of truth and justice. If, then, everything ends up justified, where is the hope?

THE HOPE THAT IS NOT SEEN

The Principle of Hope

We would do well to seek another way to approach the problem of hope. The same Jürgen Moltmann has made a great contribution in this regard with his book *Theology of Hope*.[18] As Moltmann himself acknowledges, this book resulted from the strong impact that reading Ernst Bloch's *The Principle of Hope*[19] had on him. Bloch's philosophy is important for understanding the theological innovations that appear in Moltmann. Ernst Bloch does not derive his conception of history from the general visions of history that appear in official, Soviet-style Marxism. Rather, he conceives history starting from the philosophical category of "possibility."[20] As Bloch himself reports, he takes this category from what he calls the "Aristotelian left," represented by such figures as Strato, Alexander of Aphrodisia, Avicenna, Averroes, Avicebron, Amalric of Bene, David de Diamant and Giordano Bruno. For these authors, matter is not simply a negativity that limits form, but is a primary, total potentiality on which all the possible configurations of the world depend.[21] Understood thus, historical possibility is not simply ideal possibility, in the sense of an absence of contradictions, but neither is it something already determined at the beginning of time, independently of our praxis. Possibility is a category of human praxis, insofar as this praxis looks to a future in which the *novum* awaits us, that newness in which the final content of history is anticipated.[22] Despite Bloch's reference to the Aristotelian left, it is not to be forgotten that decades earlier Martin Heidegger, in another philosophical context, had introduced the category of possibility at the moment of conceiving the historicity of human existence.[23] The introduction of the category of possibility implies a radically distinct way of viewing history.

As Xavier Zubiri showed in *Naturaleza, historia, Dios,* modern philosophy conceived of history in categories taken from natural philosophy. The Enlightenment conceived of history as the progressive development of what was already contained, from the beginning of time, in the historical subject. Whether this subject was thought of as the "human race," "Spirit," or "Matter," in every case the future of history was already potentially contained in the beginning of time. History therefore was nothing more than the unfolding of what already potentially existed from the start—or, as Hegel would say, what existed in the mind of God before creating the world. History is thus conceived with the category of potency. But this conception of history neglects the most historical aspect of history itself, which is the appearance in it of novelty. Indeed, the difference between Cro-Magnon humans and present-day humans is not their *potencies*, but their *possibilities*. The natural potencies are the same; what changes between the first humans and others are our possibilities. In this way, history appears as a process of the discovery, appropriation and handing on of possibilities. Possibilities are what the past hands on to us. But the possibilities, though they come from the past, are intrinsically directed toward the future. They are possibilities of what we are going to do.[24]

In contrast to what happens with the category of potency, history viewed from the category of possibility appears as a process open to the newness of what has not been predetermined from the beginning of time. Of course, the past conditions us, since it determines what our possibilities are. Nonetheless, nothing in the past or in the present determines what the future will be. The future is open, as threat or as promise. Jürgen Moltmann's *Theology of Hope* starts precisely from this premise: the future is not there before us, as something we can possess or know simply from our experience of the present.[25] But precisely because of that, the future and the present are not easily harmonized in a general vision of history in which all the miseries of history are easily legitimated. In Christian hope, the future stands in contradiction to the present. While the present is characterized by injustice, sin, suffering and death, what is expected in the future is precisely justice, reconciliation, happiness and the fullness of life.[26] Even so, Christian hope does not refer to a utopia alien from this world or to a paradise situated exclusively in the beyond. Christian hope is a hope for this history of ours, because it is a *possibility* of that history, already anchored in the present. Precisely because real history consists in a dynamic that empowers possibility, hope refers in a realistic way to this world and what this world can come to be, according to God's promises.[27]

Hope in Moltmann

We must be aware, nonetheless, that God's promises surpass what history can give of itself, according to its own dynamism. God's promises refer, ultimately, to a reign of God in which all sickness, all injustice and all suffering will be abolished; and in which death itself will definitively disappear. The resurrection of Jesus, as an eschatological irruption of the last times, shows the radicality of the Christian hope in a new creation. Christian hope includes the resurrection of the dead and the reconciliation of the entire creation with God. Precisely because of the radical newness of what is hoped for, the kingdom of God cannot be conceived without God, as Bloch would have it. If the future could be deduced from the potencies inherent in the original matter, then there would be no need for God. But precisely because the future is not programmed in the past, precisely because a radical newness is hoped for, the kingdom can only be of God.[28] In this sense, it appears that Bloch never freed himself completely from Aristotelianism; rather, within the Aristotelian category of potency, he simply opted for that aspect which appeared more capable of including the progressive, dialectical humanization of nature. This humanization included, of course, free human action, so that we are not dealing with a purely mechanical conception of history. Nonetheless, all the world's possible configurations are already contained for Bloch in the original matter.[29] By contrast, Moltmann's theology encompasses a conception of history in which newness radically surpasses any possible predetermination, even dialectical, at the beginning of time. The kingdom of God, to which the church is constitutively oriented, is indeed a radical newness, situated in a future that comes from God, not from our own possibilities.[30]

Certainly, Moltmann's subsequent work on *The Crucified God* moderates to some extent the optimism of his *Theology of Hope* with regard to immediate political possibilities. But he does not as a result reject this historical conception of hope; rather, it becomes more radical. Christian hope is grounded in the opposition between God and the world, which is shown on the cross, but also in the infinite mercy and nearness of God, which the cross reveals to us.[31] In this way, Moltmann's theology certainly represents an enormous contribution toward a theology that would conceive of hope

within the historical horizon of our time. Jesus' radical orientation toward the kingdom of God has been embraced, not as the
simple, naive belief of a first-century Jew facing the immediate
end of history, but as an essential characteristic of Christian faith,
which does not live for the present but for a future in which the
newness of God awaits us. The content of the future kingdom of
God shows us that this future is not something completely alien to
the hopes of the Enlightenment for a progressive improvement of
humankind. Neither is it alien to the desires of all people of good
will who long for a future where injustice, suffering and death no
longer have the only word. In contrast to modern philosophy and
liberal theology, however, Moltmann has been able to show that
this future kingdom of God, precisely because it is not deducible
from an analysis of the present or the past, is in contradiction to
that present and that past and confronts them both critically. It is
no longer possible to legitimize the present in the name of general
visions of the totality of history. The kingdom of God is *of God*,
and therefore awaits us in a future that belongs only to God.

As is well known, many of these intuitions passed over to liberation theology, though liberation theology added some accents
of its own. On the one hand, liberation theology was more concerned with analyzing in greater detail the reality of that present
which stands in contrast with the newness of the kingdom of God,
and which liberation theology has called the "anti-kingdom." On
the other hand, liberation theology has especially stressed that the
poor are the destined heirs of that kingdom, as is proclaimed in
the beatitudes (Mt 5:3; Lk 6:20). It is obviously not a question of
two independent dimensions. The reality of the anti-kingdom is
what creates poverty and keeps poor people in their suffering. For
that very reason the coming of the kingdom of God is something
that primarily concerns those who suffer most directly under the
power of the anti-kingdom.[32] These are affirmations that can be
found in Moltmann himself,[33] though he has rejected some aspects of liberation theology. Possibly his major difficulties with
that theology have to do with the "progressive" clericalism that
keeps poor people in a situation of dependence, or with the possible relapse of liberation theology into those tendencies, common
in liberal theology, to accept too naively the "hope that is seen,"
characteristic of the Enlightenment vision of history.[34]

THE FIRST FRUITS OF HOPE

The Kingdom as Reign

We are not going to enter here into the disagreement between Moltmann and liberation theology. Rather, what we are interested in stressing at this moment is a limitation in Moltmann's argument that is also present in liberation theology, and even in the "social gospel" of Rauschenbusch. All these theologies have made important efforts to recover the historicity of the kingdom of God, as it appears in scripture. They have recovered the kingdom of God as a historical reality coming from the future, and they have recovered also the contrast between that future and the "social sin" that appears massively in the present. Nonetheless, there is a decisive aspect of the kingdom of God that still has not been systematically recovered: the character of "reign," and not just "kingdom." In the Biblical conception, both in the Old and the New Testaments, the *malkut yahweh* or the *basileía toû theoû* does not refer primarily to a state or a situation, but to the fact that God reigns.[35] From a canonical point of view, the first allusion to the reign of God appears right after the drowning of Pharaoh's armies in the Reed Sea. Precisely because the people of Israel has been freed from the sovereignty of Pharaoh, Moses is able to proclaim that the Lord "reigns forever and ever" (Ex 15:18). The expression can also be translated in the future ("will reign"), but in either case it proclaims the beginning, in the present time, of something new: *the Pharaoh no longer reigns; it is God who reigns.*

It is important to observe that this reign can be proclaimed already in the desert, before the people have received the law and the land. The reign of God is, above all, the fact of God's reigning, even before that reign has been translated into a social and political situation of stability and justice. Freedom from Pharaoh's sovereignty suffices, in order to be able to proclaim the beginning of God's reign. There can be a reign of God without law and without the exercise of territorial sovereignty. Still, there is something concrete that the reign of God requires inexorably: a people. God reigns when God acquires a people and frees that people from Pharaoh's sovereignty. Of course, the fact that God reigns implies a new situation, in which there is no justice or oppression. The people over whom God reigns is a people of brothers and sisters, among whom poverty and exploitation are banished. The whole Mosaic law, in its diverse historical interpretations, effectively demonstrates this. Of course, both the introduction of the monarchy (1 Sam 8) and the capture of Jerusalem by the Babylonian empire will cast into doubt the reign of God over his people. The conception of that reign, however, will also be expanded to include God's sovereignty over all history: the successive bestial empires will ultimately be subordinated to God's rule, which will be made visible in a renewed people of Israel (Dan 7). All of this obviously implies the idea that God himself is going to reign again in person over his people, unseating the false rulers who have gained control of the people and led them to ruin (Ez 34).

All of Jesus' preaching about the kingdom presupposes these experiences of the Hebrew people.[36] When Jesus announces the imminent arrival of the reign of God, he uses, among others, the parable of the farmer who has left his vineyard—classic symbol of Israel—in the hands of tenants. The coming of the reign of God is the coming of God in person, who comes to reclaim God's people and to free them from the evil managers (Mk 12:1-12). Other similar images are the sudden return of the bridegroom to the awaiting virgins, the return of the master whom his servants weren't expecting and the return of the absent ruler. In each case the theme is similar: God returns to reign in person, dispensing with unfaithful intermediaries. To be sure, this kingdom of God is a future reality, but it is also so imminent that it is already beginning to materialize, though not always in a plainly visible manner. Its beginnings may be humble, but in the end the reign of God will be a splendorous reality, visible to all (Mk 4:30-32). These humble beginnings are not purely interior or spiritual. They are already present, now, in the community of Jesus' disciples: "the reign of God does not come with your careful observation, nor will people say 'Here it is,' or 'There it is,' because the reign of God is in the midst of you" (Lk 17:20-21). God is already reigning in history over the disciples of Jesus. As we will see further on, this raises the question of the role of Jesus in that reign. In fact, the healing activity of Jesus is an indication that the reign of God has already arrived for Israel (Mt 12:28).[37]

The Limits of the Classical Theology of the Kingdom

This dynamic dimension of the kingdom, understood as a reign exercised effectively by God, hardly appears in the classical theology of the kingdom. Both in Moltmann's theology and in liberation theology, the reign of God is understood primarily as a situation, as a state of affairs characterized by justice and peace. And, naturally, these are essential characteristics of the reign of God, which requires a situation different from that of the "anti-kingdom," in which God does not exercise dominion. Still, the new state of affairs is incomprehensible unless in fact God is effectively reigning. To be sure, Moltmann insists that the kingdom is *of God*, but he does so to emphasize that the newness that is hoped for in the future does not derive from the potencies of the past, but involves the saving action of God. This kingdom of God, however, understood as authentic newness, continues to be conceived as a future state of affairs, which God keeps introducing into history. The reign of God is not the effective exercise of sovereignty, which already exists in the present, but is a future state of affairs that cannot be realized except with the help of God.[38]

In fact the dynamic terminology, which translates *basileía toû theoû* with "reign", "sovereignty" or "dominion" of God, was not fully integrated into theological discourse. Initially Moltmann associates the idea of "dominion" or "lordship" (*Gottesherrschaft*) with the existentialist theologies, in which the reign of God had been reduced to an "eschatological conditioning of a human being's existence by the absolute exigency" of God.[39] In this way the kingdom of God is reduced to an individual reality on the margins of history. Further on, Moltmann explains that the term "dominion" has negative political connotations that offend feminist sensibilities and suggest some type of theocracy; he thus prefers to avoid it.[40] The term "reign" is initially accepted as a complement to "kingdom." According to Moltmann, the "reign" would designate the present sovereignty of God, still hidden and conflictive, while the "kingdom" would refer to the future consummation of that sovereignty, when God rules in a clear, universal and indisputable way. The reign would refer to historical immanence, while the kingdom would designate the transcendence of a reality to come.[41] Nonetheless, it is not clear why the term "reign" cannot designate both aspects, historical as well as transcendent. In fact, Moltmann does seek a term that can encompass the two dimensions, but finds it in the idea of a "new creation" which irrupts already into the present, through God's regenerating and life-giving actions.[42] This does not mean, however, a definitive rejection of the use of the expression "kingdom of God." This expression obviously continues to appear in Moltmann's theology, while Moltmann comments that the term "reign" is not appropriate in pastoral use, since it might suggest "the rumors about kings and princesses that we read in certain broadsheets."[43]

The precaution with regard to the idea of a *present* reign of God has deeper and more understandable roots in Moltmann's theology. Moltmann recognizes that the future "reign" of God has anticipations in history, and that these anticipations involve an effective "reigning" of God over his people. To quote him directly: "God reigns through the word and faith, through the promise and hope, through prayer and obedience, through force and the Spirit."[44] The difficulty for Moltmann is that from this theme of historical anticipations can arise the tendency to identify the church with the kingdom of God: the kingdom is proclaimed as already realized in the ecclesiastical institutions, and hope for the future is thus canceled out. This can happen in what Moltmann calls "ecclesiastical chiliasm." It is what happens when a church proclaims itself in a triumphant way as the perfect society, ruled over by Jesus Christ, no matter how little its internal structures reflect the fraternity, justice, equality and liberty that are proper to the reign of God.[45] If this sounds a little "catholic," it must not be forgotten that the same danger can be found in "evangelical" form, wherever a group of people "moralize" the kingdom of God and identify it with the people who submit to God and do God's will. But the kingdom of God belongs to the future, as is demonstrated by the fact that in these groups there continues to exist sickness and death.[46] The Christian community can also be turned into a therapeutic group, interested solely in itself and turning its back on the dramas of human history. All these possible errors in the churches, easily detectable throughout history, incline Moltmann to understand the Christian community as an agent working in history in favor of the kingdom hoped for from God; he does not conceive it so much as a realm over which God effec-

tively reigns already in the present time, even with the understanding that this reign has not yet reached its culmination.[47]

No doubt there are important reasons for this position, which
we will have to consider more in detail, but first it would be worth-
while to look at some important consequences of not considering
the kingdom of God as a *reign*. On the one hand are the christological consequences. The titles that primitive Christianity applied
to Jesus have obvious references to God's reign. For example, the
titles of "Messiah" (in Hebrew) or "Christ" (in Greek), which
mean the "Anointed One," refer directly to the ceremony of in-
stalling someone as *king* of Israel. The title of "Lord" (*kýrios*) for
Christ, although it translates into Greek the unpronounceable name
of God, was also the normal designation for rulers in the Hellenistic world (Acts 25:26). One of the apparently more mysterious
titles, that of "Son of Man," also contains a reference to the reign
of God. The title appears in the Book of Daniel, after the por-
trayal of the world empires that succeed one another in history
like *bestial*, inhuman realities. Opposite them appears a "son of
man" on whom God bestows power, glory and dominion over all
the peoples (Dan 7:13-14). The Hebrew expression means simply
"man," "human being," and emphasizes the *human* character of
the reign of God, in contrast to the inhuman empires. When this
type of title is applied to Jesus, it signifies that he is effectively
exercising his reign over a people. To say that Jesus is the Christ,
the Lord, the Son of Man, is to affirm that the final stage of history has begun, because the Messiah has already come, and already in the present time there appears a people to claim him as
their king. In other words, the reign of God, announced by Jesus
as an imminent reign, has already begun in history. Other New
Testament expressions, such as those that affirm the raising of
Jesus "to the right hand of the Father" (Acts 7:56, etc.) quite obviously allude to an enthronement which confers on Jesus the exercise of the reign.

The early Christian communities could say this plainly, because
they believed that in fact Jesus, dead and risen, was a living person, effectively exercising the reign of God over them, his people.
Now when the reign of God is turned into a future reign, the
christological titles lose their historical sense and tend to become
ontological terms, aimed more at explaining who Jesus *is*,[48] and

not so much what Jesus *does* in history, no matter how decisive this doing is for determining who Jesus is, as we shall see. Moltmann has doubtless attempted, as few others have, to recover the messianic character of Christology. Nonetheless, given his conception of the reign as kingdom, the messianism of the Messiah is deprived of historical concreteness in the present. Having turned the reign into *kingdom,* it is obvious that no present-day people can legitimately present itself as the *kingdom* of God. Any identification of a church or an empire with the *kingdom* would mean destroying hope for a different future for humanity. Thus in the present time it is only possible to detect situations that in some way resemble or make present the future kingdom of God, understood as that state of affairs in which all creation will be consummated and all injustice, oppression and suffering will disappear. Without doubt, we then have a magnificent transforming of the entire creation into the "new creation," which is already breaking into the present. All this is of course true and very important. According to this view, however, the Messiah, raised up and enthroned in order to exercise the *reign* of God in present-day history, disappears and becomes a cosmic Christ who leads the entire universe toward its fullness. The messianic loses its present historicity in favor of the future of creation.[49]

The first Christian communities understood themselves as the people of the Messiah, as that realm of history over which God exercises God's reign, and thus the place where the signs of that reign begin to become visible. It was not only a question of the gifts of the Spirit or the curing of infirmities. These communities experienced the disappearance of social differences between Greeks and Jews, between slaves and free, between men and women. In these communities hunger and poverty disappeared, and the communist utopias of antiquity came to be realized in a free and efficacious way (Acts 2:42-47; 4:32-37; 2 Cor 8:1-24; etc.). Of course all of this was not achieved without limitations and conflicts, as those same communities bear witness to us. But it was done precisely as an expression of the truth that the reign of God was already being exercised over history by means of the Messiah. Certainly, *these communities never thought that they were the kingdom of God; they simply thought that God was exercising God's reign over them.* And of course they never thought that history had its end in them; they believed only that their limited accomplishments were simply the first fruits of a future in which the reign of the Messiah would become visible for all humanity. Precisely for that reason, they never considered the proclamation of Jesus as Messiah as related only to the people that God had formed from among all the nations, but as something relevant for all of creation. Indeed, the particularity of the history of salvation, which always occurs through the choice and liberty of concrete individuals and communities, is in no way foreign to the entire creation. Quite the contrary: creation groans, longing to be welcomed into the glorious liberty of the children of God (Rom 8:21).

When theology loses sight of the truth that the kingdom of God is a reign, and that that reign requires a people, the result can only be an absurd opposition between the historical Jesus and the Christ of faith, or between the kingdom preached by Jesus and the message of the first Christian communities. Thus, for example, we are told that the first Christian communities "de-Messianized" Jesus, for their practical accomplishments came to be seen as subsequent to faith, as related to communities and not to a people, and as lacking a prophetic aspect oriented toward the poor.[50] This type of prejudice arises from a mistaken understanding of the relation between faith and practice, as if faith were possible "before" practice and independently of it. And of course there is a failure to understand that the Christian communities, *just like Israel*, did not understand themselves as anything more than a people destined to anticipate in history what God wants for all humanity. That means, among other things, a people destined to anticipate in history such a disappearance of poverty that there is no longer necessary a prophetic function to denounce the chosen people's infidelity to their mission in history. If in the New Testament there is no condemnation of the existence of the poor among the people of God, it is not because the poor did not matter, but because there were none. This is the reason for the absence in the first Christian communities of prophecy like that of Israel. The difference between the people of Israel, whom the prophets addressed, and the people of God assembled in communities through all the earth is precisely that the latter people is a people restored, fed and organized by Jesus.[51] In reality, the true de-Messianization of Christ did not take place in the first Christian communities, which were precisely those that proclaimed Jesus as Messiah (Christ). The de-Messianization happens rather when those communities disappear from history. Because if there is no people, neither is there a reign of God. Then the reign becomes a simple future utopia, an expression of the dreams of all people, but with no concreteness in the real historical realm over which God genuinely exercises the first fruits of God's sovereignty.

These first fruits are very important for hope. Moltmann has helped us understand that a hope that can be seen is not hope, but rather a theological legitimization of the totality of history. Nonetheless, *a hope without first fruits is not hope either.* A hope that cannot be seen at all tends to become a simple future utopia, incapable of presenting itself as an alternative for the present, as an alternative visible and realizable from this very moment, not only in the future. If Christian communities become service agencies of a future kingdom of God, certainly we will have avoided the danger of confusing the church with the kingdom, but the future reality will still remain without first fruits in the present. And without first fruits, as modest as they may be, the mission of the churches to serve the future consummation of the kingdom becomes subject to question. For how will they be able to require that the powers of this world realize in their realms of sovereignty that which the Christian communities do not realize in their own midst? Certainly the present reign of God points to an eschatological culmination; certainly that reign is not for a few select people, but is directed toward the whole of humanity and all creation. But for that to be possible, it is necessary that the liberty of the children of God, for which all creation groans, be visible, even in some quite modest way, somewhere in history. Otherwise there is no hope for creation (Rom 8:18-25).

THE STRUCTURE OF CHRISTIAN HOPE

By recovering the biblical vision of the reign of God, nineteenth- and twentieth-century theologies have made an important contribution to our ability to conceive of hope in a historical way. In Moltmann's theology we have seen an attempt to conceive of hope starting from the possibilities of human praxis, rather than in a theoretical vision of the whole of history. This perspective, which avoids legitimizing the present in the name of the totality, is nonetheless limited by a static understanding of the reign of God. Such limitations invite us to go beyond the theology of the past century, to elaborate a systematic conception of hope that will allow us both to adopt the achievements and to overcome the defects of that theology.

The Possibilities of Praxis

The concept of praxis usually provokes ambiguous reactions and even passionate dismissals, possibly due to some type of political association that forgets the long history of this term in Western philosophy. Let us say briefly that praxis means here the whole complex of human acts, which make things present to us in radical otherness and which form among themselves diverse types of more or less complex structures.[52] Thus praxis as we understand it is different both from the Aristotelian concept of praxis and from the Marxist concept. Praxis, insofar as it includes all human acts, is not opposed to productive activity, as Aristotle would have it. Such productive activity (or *poiesis)* is made up of different types of acts and therefore also belongs to praxis in the proper sense. On the other hand, praxis in our sense is not opposed to theory or contemplation, as is usually the case in Marxism. Theoretic, contemplative and indeed all intellectual acts are an integral part of praxis. In this sense, praxis comes close to meaning what in other philosophies is called "life" or "existence." But we are dealing with a concept that is even more precise. "Life" characterizes not only human beings, but also giraffes and bacteria. These, however, do not have praxis, since for them, as far as we can know, things do not become present in radical otherness; that is, they are not perceived by them as radically other.[53] For its part, "existence" is a tremendously broad term, applicable to atoms and to galaxies. When it is limited to designating the "existent" human, it becomes too narrow for our purposes, for then it means only a mode of being (Heidegger's *Dasein*), and not the acts that effectively occur in human existence.

Praxis designates, in this sense, the most intimate dimension of the human being, the acts that make up human performance, from the most private and hidden to the most public and effective. Praxis is not something simply external to human being; rather it is human being in its most radical dimension: its "life," its "existence." For this very reason praxis is not something opposed to faith; rather faith itself is an act, and as such forms part of praxis, conferring a special character on the practical structures within which it is integrated. Furthermore, praxis is not something foreign to human history; rather human history emerges precisely from one of the fundamental structures of human praxis. History, as we saw, involves acts that appropriate possibilities. This appropriation of possibilities is what formally defines the practical structure that we call "activity": human activity is the appropriation of possibilities. This appropriation of possibilities has of course individual aspects, according to which each individual keeps creating his or her own biography, but it also has a social, collective character. The properties of present-day humanity are defined by the possibilities that past human activity has bestowed on it, and the possibilities of the future will be determined by the properties that we appropriate today as individuals and as collectivities. If praxis defines a radical dimension of the human being, and if history belongs constitutively to this praxis, then history is shown to be an essential dimension of our human condition, not an external addition or some happening that is foreign to our personal reality.

Our present possibilities are defined by the realities surrounding us in the present and by the possibilities that others have appropriated in the past. Nevertheless, the appropriation of possibilities looks toward the future, toward what things could be. "Things" has here the widest possible meaning, because it is not a question only of what material things could be, but also of what other persons and you yourself could be. The possibilities that we can appropriate include the possibilities of everything around us, as well as our own possibilities, the possibilities of our own praxis. Naturally, these possibilities do not exist in the air, as simple logical possibilities, but in the reality of things, of other people, of ourselves. They are "real" possibilities and not simply a logical absence of contradiction. Thus the knowledge of our possibilities is always and simultaneously knowledge of the reality of things, of others and of ourselves. Conversely, the knowledge of things, of others and of ourselves is always and at once knowledge of

what possibilities are offered—to things, others and ourselves—
for acting in the future. An example of this is the intimate union
between scientific knowledge and the technical possibilities that it
offers. If we include under the term "reason" all the intellectual acts
that ask about the profound reality of things, others and ourselves,
it becomes clear that reason is always and simultaneously reason
about ourselves and reason about things. It is reason about things
because it shows us the profound structure of their reality; it is reason about ourselves because knowledge of the profound structure
of any reality shows us the possibilities that that reality offers us.[54]

Each present situation is defined by a system of possibilities.
These possibilities can be presented to us either as anxiety-causing
or as hopeful. When anxiety reigns, the sphere of possibilities of
acting without renouncing our desires and interests tends to become ever more restricted. Possibilities can appear, though, that
break the cycle of anxiety and allow us to hope for a situation that
will improve the present one. Thus the struggle between anxiety
and hope always has an intellectual dimension that asks about all
our possibilities. Precisely for that reason, this struggle, carried to
its ultimate consequences, causes us to ask questions about our
own ultimate possibilities, and about the ultimate possibilities that
the world can offer us. However, these possibilities can sometimes
be presented as incapable of offering us hope. Are loneliness, old
age, illness and death the ultimate possibility of our life? Is social
and ecological catastrophe the ultimate possibility of present-day
humanity? Are destruction and eternal night the final destiny of
our planet, of the solar system, of the universe? As more or less
rational as each of these possibilities might appear to be, humanity
does not stop trying to sketch out in response *alternative* possibilities that loosen the grip of anxiety and allow some type of hope.
Nonetheless, these hopeful possibilities can, in many cases, collide
with what seems rational. How, then, can we hope? Are there reasons to hope when our knowledge of the world's reality and of our
own reality seems to make hoping difficult, and even impossible?

Hope as Law

There is an aspect of our practice that allows us to ground a
certain hope. It is what we can call the "regularity" or "lawful-

ness" of human praxis. Certain types of action yield certain results: from such simple relationships as corporal movements and the impact they have on the things around us, to the most complex and technical structures. All scientific and technical treatment of the things around us supposes the possibility of discovering predictable relationships between our actions and their results. The very idea of a scientific "experiment" implies that certain of our interventions upon natural things, given defined invariable conditions, produce regularly the same results. Without such correspondences between our actions and their results, neither scientific knowledge of the world nor technical transformation of it would be possible. The human sciences, though they function of necessity with the very wide margins of probability and require the use of statistical approximations, also presuppose certain regularities in human praxis. It is thus possible, for example, to foresee that, all else being equal, a lowering of interest rates implies an increase in inflation, etc. Without such regularities not only the social sciences, but even our daily life, would be impossible. Only because we know of certain regularities (the greeting is answered, the switch turns on the light, etc.) is it possible to organize meaningfully our daily praxis in the context of a given culture.

These correspondences often have a moral character, as the very terms "law" or "rule" (*regula*) indicate. There are physical laws, but also laws and rules with respect to what is good and bad in daily life. The same applies to the adjectives and adverbs that describe our praxis. It can be said that someone who has observed certain socially accepted moral norms has acted "well." But it can also be said that someone who knows how to run a machine correctly performs "well." Certainly, the correct running of a machine is immediately shown in the results: its purposes are achieved, materials are correctly processed, etc. In the moral sphere, despite its radical difference from the technical, there are also correspondences. A good part of moral education, at least in childhood, uses rewards and punishments to stimulate certain actions and discourage others. The child who behaves well is rewarded; the one who does not is punished. Such behavior, of course, never disappears from social praxis. We always have fines and jails for offenders. We also use the simple smile as a means in daily life for sanctioning behaviors or opinions which deviate from the norm.

Conversely, those who act in accord with society's rules can expect to be accepted, esteemed, admired and rewarded in various ways by members of their social group. Of course, there are areas of human life where technical and moral correspondences are linked together: an economy minister may have acted "badly" from the viewpoint of certain economic "laws," but the minister's action may also have left thousands of persons unemployed, and this implies certain ethical and political responsibilities. The minister therefore deserves some type of political or juridical sanction. This is the most elemental meaning of justice: to give to people their due, so that things will go well for those who act well, and things will go badly for those who act badly.

Given then the existence of such regularities, there appears a certain way of grounding hope. I can believe that if in the different situations of my life I appropriate the possibilities that are "good" and "correct" from a moral or technical viewpoint, then I will obtain the hoped for results. Those things that I desire will get realized, and my hopes will find a certain degree of fulfillment. Thus I know what I have to do to reach my goals. The correspondence between certain actions and their results, the lawfulness or regularity that appears in human praxis, is what grounds my hopes. Of course, we realize that the most elaborate technical constructs can come crashing down because of an unexpected accident, which puts a tragic end to entire chains of foreseen and hoped for regularities. We also know that moral behaviors do not always earn the praise of one's fellows, but rather meet with rejection and persecution. The plans of the just can fail. Misfortune, accidents, illnesses and death seem to put to the test any hope built on the regularities of our praxis. At such times, we try to compensate for this fragility of praxic regularities by some type of metaphysical or religious consideration. A certain "fundamental confidence" in the world, or a certain belief in the divine, can makes us trust that, despite everything, *in the end all will turn out well for the just.* The sufferings that the just pass through now are no more than "tests" or struggles in which their mettle is made manifest, because in the end all will turn out well for them. When death appears finally to put an end to all hope, metaphysical or religious considerations can still defend the existence of a great beyond where definitive rewards and punishments will be handed out, thus assuring that no good and no evil will be left without its corresponding desert. God or the gods then guarantee that for the just person, it will go well in this world or in the world to come, and that for the evil person sooner or later it will go badly.

Having reached this point, we can now understand that "hope as law" is the ultimate secret of the "hope that is seen." Indeed, the idea that certain regularities allow us to foresee the future consequences of our own actions implies in the final analysis a conception of history, namely, that history is the realm in which the increase of technical knowledge, accompanied by correct moral behavior, guarantees the future success of our own actions. For those who possess the correct knowledge and act accordingly, all goes well; for those who refuse to be enlightened, it goes badly. For those who act morally, all goes well; for those who act badly from an ethical point of view, it goes badly. The ignorant and the wicked are the losers of history. In this way, history appears as continual progress both in mastery over nature and in the moral perfecting of humanity. From the theological viewpoint, God may appear as the ultimate guarantor of these processes. Otherwise, different entities, more or less "divine," may take on the same guaranteeing function: Spirit, Nature, Matter, Humankind, etc. They make it possible for us to believe that this world, despite all its apparent misfortunes, is ultimately well-made. Those who act correctly (the enlightened and the honest) can be sure that in the end all will go well for them. Such a view, as we have seen, implies a tremendous legitimization of everything that happens in history. The hope that is seen is not hope, but a wholesale legitimization of the present in the name of a future justice.

The praxic perspective allows us to discern more deeply how pernicious is this view of hope, for if things go well for the good and badly for the evil, this implies a reading of history in which those for whom things go badly *are* the evil ones, and those for whom things go well *are* the good ones. If things go well for you, it is because you deserve it. Your ability, your knowledge, your moral stature have made it possible. If things go badly for you, you must have done something wrong. Insofar as this perspective is open to theological considerations, God is the one who ultimately sanctions the well-being of the powerful and the misery of the poor. In a just world, created and sustained by God, each person gets his or her deserts. This is the deepest of all ideologies, one declared and expounded continually in all those stories in which the good, after passing through diverse trials, finally emerge triumphant, while the evil, despite their initial successes, are finally punished. But it is something more than an ideology. It is an intentional schema that orients and structures human praxis in society. It therefore has enormous practical effects. Paul Krugman, an economist at the Massachusetts Institute of Technology, has observed that so-called "neoliberalism," precisely because it cannot guarantee the well-being of all humanity, must necessarily proclaim that the poor are to blame for their own situation.[55] Through their ignorance, their exotic culture, their resistance to implementing policies imposed on them by other countries, etc., they make themselves culpable for their own misfortune. Antón Costas, professor of economic policy at the University of Barcelona, has observed that the main reason why half the world is still in poverty is "a strong tendency in human nature" to think that both the poor and the rich deserve their respective situations. This tendency, which we have seen here to be rooted in "hope as law," makes possible our easy acceptance of other people's misery and our uncritical self-satisfaction with our own wealth.[56] It allows the world to continue being the way it is.

It is important to note that the problem, as we have analyzed it here, does not reside simply in the possibility of finding regularities in our praxis. Without such regularities, ordinary daily life would be impossible, as would be also scientific knowledge of the world, or the appearance of any type of skill. The problem appears when these regularities become the ground for one's own hope; or, to use another theological term, when these regularities are used to justify one's own praxis. If I act correctly, things will go well for me; if they go well for me, it is because I have acted correctly. We are dealing with the theological problem of justification. Let us not forget that praxis, in our analysis, means the most radical dimension of the human being. We are therefore not speaking of the legitimization of "works" external to the human being; we are speaking of the legitimization of our life, our existence, of the most intimate aspect of ourselves, which is what we here have called "praxis." "Hope as law" is a way of legitimizing our praxis. What type of legitimization is it? It is a legitimization of the "law by works," as the Pauline expression has it (Rom 3:27). Since in our works there exist regularities, these regularities, this lawfulness, this "law," can be converted into a principle to achieve our justification. Thus it can be seen that the theological problem of justification is not a problem extraneous to history. We have already mentioned its historical dimensions, citing economists who probably do little theology. Indeed, the justification of praxis according to the schema we have just analyzed is nothing other than the ultimate legitimization of all those for whom things go well, the legitimization of all the powerful, the legitimization of the present as the ultimate meaning of history, and the final legitimization of the order of this present world as the correct one.

Hope as Promise

There exists another praxic structure in which hope appears: that of promise. Promise has a constitutively interpersonal structure, and in this sense it is radically different from law. Law does not include a constitutive reference to personal otherness. An isolated person, or a closed group, can determine alone what their possibilities are, in accord with the correspondence between actions and results. In promise, however, there appears the other, the stranger. "Promise" implies that there is someone who can say to the person or the group something that transcends their own reckoning of the possibilities of their praxis. It is not a question of the "intersubjectivity" of a group, for any isolated group can reckon "intersubjectively" the possibilities that are within their reach, in function of this correspondence between action and results. It is a question of "interpersonality," whereby the person or the group is confronted with a promise *that comes from without*. But it is not a "coming from without" in the geographical sense. It is a "coming from without" precisely because the promise contains more than the individual or the group can expect when they consider their own possibilities as such. The individual person or the group receives as promise something which they themselves cannot achieve. The conjectures about the future chains of action and results are therefore superseded. Something truly new appears on the horizon.

Something truly new appears, but it appears as *promise*. Of course, promise does not break with historicity. Promise continues to be situated *in history*, as a *possibility* that another announces for the future. Nonetheless, this possibility does not derive from capabilities that the individual or the group receiving the promise already possesses. It derives from what the other, the stranger, can do. And here some very precise structures appear. In order for the promise to be accepted as a possibility for one's own praxis, one must have *confidence* in the other, in the stranger who promises. The other promises something that eludes my future reckoning, but confidence in what the other says converts the promise into possibility for me. The other does not, for that reason, become a guarantor of correspondence between my action and its results. In promise, the future is no longer a result of my action, but a possibility that *does not depend exclusively on me*. It depends on the other, on what the other knows, on what the other has experienced, on what the other can do. For that reason we have to trust in the other's *word*. Truth here acquires a meaning very different from the one it has in "hope according to the law." According to the "law," the truth of what I hope for depends on whether my reckoning about the future *corresponds* to the structures of reality. Thus hope according to the law is a hope that is seen or that aspires to be seen. In promise, truth is before all else the *fulfillment* of the word that the other has given. In the future it will be seen whether the word of the one who has promised was solid or unreliable, whether it was true or not, whether one's own future could be built upon it or not.

Confidence with regard to the other depends in good measure on my knowledge of the other, on the experiences I have had with the other. In these experiences, the other has proved to be either worthy or unworthy of confidence. This knowledge of the other, however, has a paradoxical structure. On the one hand, to the extent that I have had past experiences with the other, my confidence is strengthened or weakened. If the other has been faithful to his word in the past, then his word becomes more worthy of confidence. His promise then presents itself as a solid possibility for my future. On the other hand, the other cannot be known exhaustively. If I know the other fully, I know what the other can do and can promise. I know why he promises it, I know if he is going to be able to realize what he promises, and I know also how he is going to realize his promises. In this case, the other ceases to be an other, a stranger. The other becomes someone who can enter into my own practical reckoning; he is one more link in the chain of my actions and the corresponding results. Hope as promise then comes to be hope according to the law; hope that is not seen becomes hope that is seen, with all its fateful consequences. The knowledge of the fidelity of the other to his promises cannot therefore be an exhaustive knowledge of the other. Now this understanding of the other, which requires sufficient *nearness* so as to ground the confidence, as well as sufficient *distance* so as to preserve the otherness of the promise, takes place in the *memory*. In memory, the past fidelity of the other to his promises is made present. Nevertheless, the memory does not exhaust the reality of the other, for no present fact allows us to calculate how the other will act. In memory, the other remains someone free and yet someone trustworthy. In memory, the other's past fidelity to his promises is open to a *future*, in which it is hoped that the other will act according to his word. Memory is linked directly with hope, not the hope that is seen, but the hope that is not seen and which for that reason is true hope.

Hope as promise appears in many aspects of human praxis. In love, the other person presents himself or herself as someone who promises to be at my side in the future. This is something that does not depend on me, but on the gratuitous gift of the other. Likewise, in determining a way of life, a human being cannot live several lives beforehand, in order to decide afterward which is best. Each person has to listen to the experiences of others who have already lived their lives, and trust what those experiences teach and promise.[57] Promise also has a theological dimension, at least, that is the experience of the religion of Israel. The Hebrew scriptures speak of a God who acts in history, who opens up new possibilities for God's people, who fulfills God's promises faithfully and abundantly. Starting from Abraham, the father of faith, who could not count on earlier experiences to sustain his confidence, the history of Israel is presented, from a theological perspective, as a history framed by the structure of promises and fulfillments.[58] The promises with regard to the future reign of God are sustained by the memory of God's past intervention, in order to wrest Israel from the sovereignty of Pharaoh. On that unforgettable occasion, the Lord God became the only sovereign of Israel, capable of providing her with a social structure based on the Torah, in which the injustices experienced in Egypt were never to be repeated. In the mind of Israel, this memory is a source of hope not only for the chosen and liberated people, but for all the nations for which Israel would fulfill a universal function: none other than that of demonstrating, from this very moment, what happens in history when a people is governed by God. The reversals suffered in the course of history do not mean for Israel a failure of hope, but rather serve as the occasion for transferring that hope to a future in which the reign of God reaches all people, in a creation definitively liberated from injustice, suffering and oppression.

We should keep in mind, nonetheless, that in Israel, hope-as-promise does not do away completely with hopes based on the law. In fact, the law of Israel, consisting in an "instruction" (torah) on the new relationships with one's neighbors and with God that appear under God's sovereignty, can come to be used as a means for reckoning one's own future. The fulfillment of the law can be interpreted as the means necessary for the divine promises to be fulfilled. If the people fulfill the law, they will be able to count on God's blessings; if they do not fulfill it, they will be abandoned by the true ruler of Israel and will suffer oppression at the hands of the empires. In this way the people's misfortunes can come to be interpreted as the punishment they deserve for their infidelity to the law. Certainly the religion of Israel is aware that the saving initiative comes from God and not Israel, so that grace is not something that can be obtained through one's own merits. But it *is* something that can be lost when the law is not fulfilled (Deut 28:1-68, etc.).[59] The sacrifices, especially the expiatory sacrifices, aim to regain the divine favor when one is aware of one's transgressions, or when various misfortunes make one aware that a transgression has been committed. One inflicts on oneself the damages deserved, and thus the original relationship with God is restored.[60] Consequently, there appears in Israel an ambiguity between the hope based on the law and the hope based on the promises. The Christian reading of the Old Testament emphasizes, nonetheless, this latter hope, because it points toward the arrival—through an anointed king, the Messiah descended from David—of a promise that surpasses all deserving. It is the promise of a new reign of

God in the final stage of history, where violence and oppression will be definitively overcome.

Christ, Our Hope

The New Testament calls Christ "our hope" (1 Tim 1:1), applying to him an attribute that the Old Testament had applied to God (Ps 71:7; Jer 14:8; 17:13). This designation of Christ as the hope of Christians is possible by virtue of a double movement. First, Christ manifests the incompatibility between the God of Israel and all hope founded on the logic of the law—that is, all hope founded on the principle of a correspondence between our actions and their results. Second, in Christ hope-as-promise finds a decisive fulfillment: the reign of God has drawn close to history and is already present in history, as much as its full realization still awaits us in the future. The Pauline expression according to which Christ is "the end of the law" (Rom 10:4) encompasses in some way both of these dimensions. On the one hand, the law ceases to function as a way to ground a hope that is seen: this is so not only for the Torah of Israel, but for every instance that can be used to found hope on the correspondence between our actions and their results. On the other hand, however, Christ is the end to which the Torah of Israel had always pointed, because in Christ are fulfilled the promises of a reign of God in which poverty, inequality, violence and oppression would disappear. Let us examine this in more detail.

On the one hand, Christ represents the end of every pretension of grounding hope in the verifiable correspondences between our actions and their results. In some religions, the gods are understood as those who guarantee that correspondence: for the just it will go well; for the unjust it will go badly. Now the incredible aspect of Christian faith is the affirmation that *the one who supposedly was to be the guarantor of that correspondence is the same one who hangs on the cross.* The religion of Israel declared that everyone who is hung on a tree is accursed (Deut 21:23; Gal 3:13). Christian faith affirms that the one who is hung on a tree is none other than God in person, who in Christ was reconciling the world with himself (2 Cor 5:19). This is a matter of true reconciliation, which proclaims as just those whom history has declared abandoned by God. In the abandonment of Jesus on the cross, God's trinitarian unity is realized. By identifying with Christ, God takes on the fate of all those who are presumed to be rejected by God. At the same time, however, a universal pardon is offered on the cross, because it proclaims that God does not take account of our offenses. The idea of a God who is ready to recompense each person according to his or her deserts has been nullified on the cross (Col 2:14). In this way God leaves without effect every pretension of self-justification by the results of one's own actions, and every hope based on a reckoning of correspondences. Indeed, what God has done on the cross surpasses every possible expectation based on our reckonings. We find ourselves before the incredible truth of a God who is radically handed over to us.

On the other hand, in Christ the reign of God irrupts anew into history, in such a way that the messianic promises begin to be fulfilled. The praxis of Jesus reveals the beginning of the messianic times, the moment when Israel's aspirations for the future and for all humanity begin to be realized: the blind see, the deaf hear, the lame walk, the sick are cured and the poor have the good news announced to them (Mt 11:5). This good news includes the dwelling of Jesus amidst a people who are learning to be "discipled," organized and fed. New social relationships, outside the dominant system, begin to appear around Jesus (Mk 6:35-44) and they are relationships already free of the logic of the law. Indeed, Jesus' acts of healing show that a new reconciling power has irrupted into history. The sick can no longer be considered to be abandoned by God; rather they appear now as the privileged object of God's attention. Jesus Christ is good news for all the poor, to whom the reign of God now appears to be especially directed, not only because the praxis of Jesus nullifies the logic of the law, which declared them accursed, but also because that praxis creates new social relationships, in which inequality and domination disappear. Among the disciples of Jesus, who renounce their possessions to share them with others, the irruption of the reign of God becomes manifest. This irruption acquires a radical character with the resurrection of Jesus from the dead. If God was in Christ, death could not hold him. The end of time has thus already begun, with Jesus as the first fruits of the new creation. Resurrected, he is the first member of a new humanity. Moreover, as resurrected, he is no longer a simple memory, but someone alive and present in the reconstituted community of his followers.

The Christian community proclaims this resurrected Jesus as Messiah, as the Christ, the one anointed by the Lord to reign over his people. If Jesus is the Anointed, it means that there is in effect a reign. If God identified completely with Jesus, then the reign of the Messiah is the reign of God. Here we are faced with a very important question, often ignored by theology. In those Old Testament texts that express a messianic hope, we find a notable ambiguity between the reign of God and the reign of the Messiah. Once the monarchy of Israel has collapsed, different strands of scripture accuse the leaders of Israel—the kings and priests—of being the ones principally responsible for the people's downfall. These kings, who in a certain way had displaced God as direct ruler of Israel (1 Sam 8), could still be understood as persons who exercised the monarchy in the name of God, and in this sense they sat "on the throne of God's reign over Israel" (1 Chron 28:5; cf. 2 Chron 13:8). In the face of the failure of these leaders, God proclaims that God, in person, will reign again over Israel. Nonetheless, these affirmations are interwoven with others, in the same biblical texts, that announce the figure of a "prince," a descendent of the house of David, sent by God to govern the people (Ez 34:1-31). The ambiguity between the idea of God exercising the reign in person, and that of a new messianic figure exercising the reign in God's name, is resolved when Christian faith proclaims that God has identified completely with Christ, who, dead and risen, now exercises the reign of God over his people.

The affirmation of the divinity of Jesus Christ does not derive from ontological speculation about the natures of Jesus, but rather from soteriology: the logic of the law could only be superseded by the identification of God with Christ, and that identification grounds the affirmation that today, in our history, the reign of God has already broken in. It is a question of historical soteriology, a soteriology that includes the reign of God. The proclamation by Jesus and by primitive Christianity, that the reign of God has drawn close to God's people and now is present in history, is credible only if in history there actually exists a people whose king, whose Messiah, is none other than God. Therefore, the identification of Christ as Messiah is not contrary either to the reign of God now present or to the divinity of Christ. The first Christians did not call Jesus "the Christ" simply to define who Jesus was ontologically. Christians call Jesus the Christ or the Messiah precisely because he is the one who today exercises the reign of God. In the same way, Christians do not call Jesus "God" simply to say that God is manifest in Jesus, or to speculate about natures and persons. Christians call Jesus God because we believe that we can be saved from the law only by a crucified God, who has suffered in person the fate of those presumably abandoned by God. And Christians call Jesus God because only if the Messiah is God, is the reign really *of God*, and not of someone who exercises it in God's place. In this sense, what Jesus *does* today (reign in the kingdom of God) is what allows us to understand who he really *is* (the Messiah or the Son of God). Other christological affirmations, such as the enthronement of Jesus in the heavens or his titles of Lord and Son of Man, are constitutively referred to the present reign of God. Because Jesus reigns as Lord in a reign that is not "beastly," but human, Jesus merits those titles with which the churches acclaim him.

The First Fruits of Hope

We have seen that, in the same way that the hope that is seen is not hope, so too the hope that is not seen *at all* is not hope either, but a simple utopia, an ideal model of what things should be, but one incapable of providing hope if we do not feel able to build it ourselves. In contrast to the hope that is not seen at all, Christian faith affirms that the first fruits of hope are already present in history through the Spirit (Rom 8:23). Paul uses the image of the pledge by which an advance is made on what is promised in a contract (2 Cor 1:22; 5:5). Now in what do these first fruits consist exactly? As we have made clear, the reign of God is not a future state of affairs, but the reality that God in person, right now, is in Christ reigning over his people. But what does this reign entail? We are obviously not dealing with a reign that is exercised through a ruler's monopoly on legitimate coercive violence over a given territory. Jesus rejected the recourse to violence, precisely because he rejected the idea of returning evil for evil, as is proper to states (Rom 13:1-7). In fact, Jesus appears to have avoided any messianic proclamation that might have made him liable to be confused with aspirants to political power in a national state. Of course, Jesus also rejected any relationships among his disciples that followed the model of states (Lk 22:24-30). In what, then, does the sovereignty of Jesus consist?

It is a question of sovereignty that is founded on *faith*, but this must be understood correctly. We are speaking of a sovereignty that is exercised over the community of faith. It is not a matter of sovereignty that is exercised only over the heart of the individual, turned toward God in solitude. Nor is it purely spiritual, foreign to history. Faith is a moment of our praxis, in the sense described above. For that reason faith is never foreign to history, which is nothing other than praxis. Now, what is it that unites faith with the reign of God, thus introducing into history the first fruits of hope? It is not a question of one's "believing in the reign of God," in the sense of believing that such a reign exists, or having hope that God will reign in the future. It is rather a question of believing in the God who has identified completely with Christ. It is faith in Christ, just as he is announced to us by the apostles, as the one who redeems the most intimate dimension of our lives, as the one who redeems our praxis. To the extent that we believe that in Christ, God's promises have been confirmed for his people (2 Cor 1:20), to that same extent we are freed from founding our hope on our reckoning of our own possibilities. We are no longer prisoners of the pretension of self-justification that is founded on the law. Our hope still awaits the redemption of this world, but still we have in our own praxis the pledge of that liberation. In faith, our praxis stays free of the pretension of self-justification and all its fateful consequences. Our praxis ceases to be "ours," in the sense that our hopes are founded on reckonings about the correspondences between our actions and their results. Our praxis belongs now to the Messiah; it is placed under his sovereignty. We enter into the realm of his reign.

It is important to note that this redemption of our praxis—the placing of our praxis under the sovereignty of the Messiah—insofar as this happens by faith, is not properly our work. Faith is a gift of God. In reality, if faith were our own work, we would not escape the logic that seeks to found hope on the reckoning of the possibilities that result from our own praxis. The pretension of self-liberation is an attempt to make the promises of God emerge from the capabilities of our own praxis. In such efforts, however, the promises cease to be promises, and history is left with only a hope that, as visible, is no longer hope. For that reason the Spirit is essential for our liberation. The Spirit is God personally transforming the most intimate moments of our praxis, making possible in that praxis the faith that opens us up to the other, to love and to hope. The reign of God belongs to the poor with Spirit, and not to those who, sure of their own possibilities, believe they can ground their hope in themselves. Of course, this work of the Spirit does not alienate us from our praxis. Praxis, no matter how situated it is beneath the sovereignty of God, no matter how transformed it is by the Spirit, does not cease to be the most intimate dimension of ourselves. Our own liberty does not disappear, and for that reason neither does the unavoidable necessity of continually evaluating our own possibilities. Christian hope is not set in opposition to human projects,[61] precisely because this hope is inserted into the heart of our praxis, placing our praxis under the sovereignty of God, but not converting it into a praxis alien to ourselves.

As we have seen, the problem does not lie in the fact that our praxis has possibilities, or that there necessarily exist correspondences between our actions and their results. The problem appears when these correspondences become the ground of our hope. When the ground of our hope consists in the promises ratified in Christ, our praxis, liberated from the pretension of self-grounding, still continues to be a free praxis. It is a new liberty, that does not consist in choosing the actions whose corresponding results can give hope to our lives, but rather in allowing the promises of God to be what justifies our hope. For we are then free of the law, not in the sense of being free of ethical requirements, but in the sense of being free of the thought that it is we ourselves who must ground our own hope. We also become free of the fear of failure, because we know that the death of Christ on the cross has absorbed all failure, proclaiming that those presumed to be abandoned by God are the very ones whose fate God personally shares through love. Even the ultimate failure of death, the wall against which all our hopes crash, has lost its daunting force. If our praxis belongs to God, not even death can separate us from the one who has led us by love into the realm of his sovereignty. Nothing, then, can separate us from Christ (Rom 8:31-39). Nothing can take from us the freedom to follow him. Nothing can take from us the full liberty of the children of God.

All these affirmations, amply described in the Christian scriptures, do not refer to heavenly events, but are destined to unfold in history. And they do unfold, if Jesus is the Messiah. Or to state it conversely: there where Jesus is the Messiah, the logic of the law disappears, and with it the logic of retributions, of competition, of envy and of violence. The logic of justifying oneself disappears, as well as the logic of the hope that is seen, because at root all such logic does no more than express the Adamic pretension to nourish oneself with the fruits of one's own actions. This supposes that there is a realm in history where pardon is exercised, where evil is not returned for evil, where self-justification is not attempted, where death is not feared, and where people enjoy the liberty, the peace and the hope that do not come from ourselves, but from the promises of God. It is a realm, therefore, where wealth can be shared. It is the place where the love of God and fraternal love make useless every pretension of power and prestige that would justify our own praxis by showing our ability to produce results. According to the testimony of the first Christian communities and of hundreds of Christians in the course of the centuries, these realms do exist, wherever people place themselves in faith under the sovereignty of the reign of God. The first fruits of hope therefore become visible in the communities that recognize Jesus as Messiah. And they become visible in all the places of history, as few in number as they may be, where the same logic of the reign takes hold, for the light of Christ illumines every human being and his Spirit is free to blow where she will.[62]

Naturally the irruption of the reign of God can more easily reveal all its possibilities when it is well known who it is who reigns and what are the conditions of that reign. This does not imply, however, an identification of the Christian churches with the reign of God. The very use of the term "reign" instead of "kingdom" safeguards the transcendence of the reign. It is God who reigns, not the church. The church is the people over whom God reigns: a people made up of sinners, a people made up of believers who must always seek help for their unbelief. Nonetheless, it is a people that recognizes Jesus as its Christ, its Messiah, its ruler. If the "kingdom" were a state of affairs, then it could be confused more easily with other states of affairs—the states of affairs in certain institutions, for instance—that in some way resemble the perfect state of affairs, in which God will be all in all. The difference would only be a matter of degree. In contrast, if the kingdom is a *reign*, exercised by God already in the present, then no confusion is possible. The reign is of God; the church is God's people. Of course, there is no reign without a people, but the people is not the reign; the reign is the simple fact that God reigns. Nevertheless, this reign, since it is a free reign, grounded in faith and not force, can in no way be a tyranny. Naturally the term "reign" can summon up connotations of tyranny. When Christians use this term, however, they do so precisely by way of contrast, to mean that they are under a new sovereignty, very different from the bestial empires that run through human history (Dan 7). It is the sovereignty of God, who makes all other sovereignty impossible by establishing a people of brothers and sisters where no one lords it over anyone else (Mt 23:8-12).

In fact, the sovereignty of God's reign is in a certain way shared. Even in the Book of Daniel, when the idea of a human government by the Son of Man is introduced, the text also indicates that the reign will be handed over to "the people of the saints of the Most High" (Dan 7:27). In the same way, Jesus speaks repeatedly of handing over the reign to his disciples, or he represents them as seated beside him on their thrones (Lk 22:29; Mt 19:28; 25:34). The Second Letter to Timothy and the Book of Revelation portray Christians as reigning together with Jesus, so that his reign is not individual, but rather a reign in which the people are priests and monarchs (2 Tim 2:12; Rev 5:10). From this follows the participation of all Christians in ministry and in the administration of the communities.[63] This sharing of the reign of Christ has deep roots in the structure of salvation. Indeed, the handing over of Jesus on the cross is precisely what makes possible the irruption of the reign of God in history. In this apparent abandonment by God there is a trusting surrender to God, through which the liberation of humanity from the Adamic logic of self-justification, from the ultimate root of all false hope, becomes possible. Jesus is then the one who, by his surrender, initiates our faith. The faith of Christians, made possible by the Spirit, is, then, nothing other than a participation in the very faith of Jesus. Christians reign with Jesus because they participate, through the Spirit, in Jesus' own relationship with God. This is just what is meant by the adoptive filiation of believers. As brothers and sisters of the elder Brother, Christians can begin new social relationships right now in history. It is the irruption of the reign of God into history.

Theological Implications

This analysis distances us in some respects from a good part of the theology of the past century. If the reign of God actually irrupts into Christian communities, then the message of Jesus about the imminence of the reign was not the simple illusion of a first-century Jew, later proved wrong by the facts. Nor can we argue that this irruption of the reign is rendered superfluous by the reality of the resurrection, as theology has proposed at times. Certainly the resurrection of Christ is an anticipation of the final destiny of humanity, but the anticipation in history of the reign of God is not exhausted in the resurrection. The reign of God requires that God reign, and therefore it requires a people. When this "reign" is reduced to a state of affairs, the resurrection in itself can be considered an anticipation of the "reign" of God, even in the absence of God's exercise of sovereignty over a people. However, the experience of the first Christian communities tells us something quite different. If they could designate Jesus as Messiah (Christ), as anointed king, it was because they experienced the risen one as someone who *was reigning* over his people, gathered together freely by faith. Otherwise, other titles, such as "savior," would have been sufficient. The proclamation of Jesus as the Christ is rooted in the recognition by the first Christian communities of the effective exercise of his sovereignty in history; this recognition is the greatest evidence of the continuity between the message of primitive Christianity and the message of Jesus. If there is any discontinuity between these two messages, it does not consist in primitive Christianity's failure to announce the reign of God; rather, it is in the belief that that reign, affirmed as a reality already present in history, is made possible by the fact that Jesus, dead and risen, is now seated at the right hand of God as the Messiah of the renewed Israel, formed by the Christian communities. The Christian communities assume in history the original mission of Israel: to be testimony to and pledge of the fraternity, the equality, the liberty and the justice to which all humanity is called.

Nor does it make any sense to contrast Jesus and the Christian communities by arguing that Jesus addressed himself to the whole people of Israel, whereas after Jesus the reign appeared to be limited to the communities. The root of this difference lies in the rejection of Jesus by the leaders of Israel, and in the appearance in the Christian communities of a people that now considered itself to be under the sovereignty of the true Messiah. When Jesus addressed himself to the people of Israel, he was not addressing himself to just another people, as he might have addressed himself to the Greeks or the Syrians. He was addressing himself to that people—chosen through Abraham and rescued from Egypt—that had the historic mission of being a city upon a hill, governed by God, in which the injustices of other peoples were not to be repeated and to which the nations would make pilgrimages. Jesus addresses himself to Israel, announcing that God returns to rule over his people, and that therefore Israel has the possibility of conversion. When the leaders of Israel reject Jesus, he concentrates on his disciples, who are considered—in the choice of twelve—to be symbolic representatives of the renewed Israel. The death and resurrection of Jesus are interpreted by these disciples as the beginning of the messianic times, in which the nations are invited to incorporate themselves into the reign of God. In this sense, the task of the disciples is *more oriented to other peoples than was the task of Jesus*, who concentrated his efforts on one final calling of Israel. Nevertheless, the mission of the apostles to the Gentiles and the formation of believing communities outside Israel by no means contradict the fact that the reign of God is directed to a people. This expanded mission means the establishment of that new people as a society over which God reigns, a society in which the justice, fraternity and equality of the messianic times have already begun.

In this sense the perception of the people of God changes, but the fact that the reign requires a people does not change. Israel is perceived by Jesus as a people for whom the reign of God is ordained, but over whom God does not reign because they have ignored God's repeated invitations. By contrast, the Christian communities understood themselves as a realm over which the Messiah was effectively reigning: in peace, justice, sharing of possessions, disappearance of poverty, attention to orphans and widows, the gifts of the Spirit, etc. In no case, however, is the people of God made equivalent to the people of Egypt or the people of Macedonia. The call of those peoples to the reign of God is necessarily mediated by the existence of a people over whom God already reigns, and in whom is manifest something interesting and attractive for all other peoples; this people is the first fruits of hope for all other peoples. The beginning of the messianic times makes it possible for the good news of the *authentic* arrival of God's reign in history to be announced to all other peoples, as an invitation to incorporate themselves now into the people of God. This invitation, nonetheless, does not make a people of God out of those who are ruled over, not by God, but by other kings and lords. Historicity always means that the universal is mediated by the particular. The blessing of all the nations of the earth always has the necessary historical mediation of particular elections (Gen 12:1-3).

This perception of the reign of God lasted for centuries in the Christian church. Sometimes the famous expression of Origen, according to which Christ is "the very kingdom" (*autobasileía*) of God, is cited as proof that the preaching of the reign of God was replaced by the preaching of Christ. One must believe that those who say this have not read Origen's text carefully. Origen comments in his text on the biblical expression "the reign of heaven is like a king who . . ." (Mt 18:23). Obviously, Matthew can compare the reign of God with what a king does, precisely because he understands *basileía* primarily as reign, not simply as kingdom. That is, a kingdom does not necessarily resemble what the king does; a reign *is* what the king does—reign. Thus Origen understands that Christ, as *autobasileía*, is not simply "the very kingdom," but "the very reign" of God. That is, Christ appears in this text of Origen as one who reigns presently and efficaciously over his own people, and one whose reign is manifest in the measure that justice, wisdom and truth take root, since his reign is exercised in this world, not only in the world to come.[64] One might criticize Origen's text for its neoplatonic dualism between matter and spirit,[65] but not for its perception of the reign of God as a reign exercised in this history of ours. Nonetheless, the conversion of Christianity into the official religion of the empire brought about some basic transformations. The reign of God had to be made compatible with the reign of the emperor. The liberty of belonging to the people of God was replaced by the obligatory profession of an imposed religion. The contrast between what happens in the realm where God reigns and what happens in the order of this world is diluted when all become believers by obligation; this dilution implies a minimalist ethics in which Christians (except for monks) are no longer asked to do more than fulfill the basic precepts of the "natural law." Non-violence and sharing possessions cease to be distinctive characteristics of believers and become rather the monastic practice of some groups of "superior" Christians. The present reign of God begins to be seen as a hidden state of affairs, as a future utopia, as a reign of the great beyond.

CONCLUSION

We began these reflections by alluding to the exhortation of the First Letter of Peter to give reasons for the hope that is in us. And we said that that exhortation was addressed to a community which, having been formed as a space for solidarity among people of rather poor background, nonetheless (or for that reason) was rejected by the larger society. This community was urged not to respond with evil against its aggressors, and at the same time was encouraged to give reasons for its hope. We can now understand the intimate relationships between these apparently unconnected exhortations. Hope that is seen is, as we have noted, hope according to the law, that is, hope grounded on the correspondence between actions and their results. According to this structure everyone receives his or her deserts, and the aggressor is opposed with aggression. Christians, on the other hand, do not respond in this way to persecutions, and this means that certainly we are no longer in hope according to the law, no longer in hope based on our own possibilities or on the possibilities of others. Ours is hope that in this sense *is not seen*. Yet, in another sense, it *is seen*, because there exists in history a fraternal community that does not return evil for evil. The hope of the community is visible to the persecutors, and precisely for that reason, it is hope for which reasons must be given. If it were not seen, there would be no need to give reasons; but since this hope is visible, acting in history, it is possible to ask about the reason for it. Since the reason is not obvious for the persecutors, it is necessary to give the reason for it.

What then is the reason (*lógos*) for the hope that exists among us? The Christian answer is that the reason is Christ. This is not merely a pious phrase, but a declaration that is rigorously coherent with the structure of hope as it is analyzable in our praxis. Through Christ hope according to the law reaches its end, with Christ God says yes to all God's promises to his people, and in Christ are already present the first fruits of the new humanity. The cross has shown that God nullifies the pretension of self-justification which places in oneself the grounding of one's hopes. The death and resurrection of Christ have shown us that God does not abandon his people, but maintains—even unto the ultimate consequences—his commitment to again draw near to them in order to initiate the promised reign. By his resurrection Christ reigns presently over his people, in whom the pledge of a new world is already visible. We do not stand before a dead Christ, nor before the glorified Christ of other theologies; we stand before the dead and risen Christ who is acting in history. This acting is still awaiting a definitive fulfillment, for the sovereignty of the Messiah is still in conflict with the powers of this world. And his very people still walks in weakness, wavering between faith in his word and the unbelief that closes in on itself. The ultimate enemy, which is death, has still not been defeated. Nonetheless, what Christian communities presently experience in history is the anticipation that one day the victory of the Messiah will reach all humanity, which sighs for it from the bottom of its heart. Then shall Christ turn over the reign to the Father, and God will be all in all.

In this sense, the future of Christianity is not at risk when the institutions of a Constantinian mold are shattered. Such a mold is shared by both left and right, in the belief that the decisive contribution of Christians for social change takes place when Christians achieve some quota of power in the palaces of the emperors. This pattern, fortunately, is coming to an end. The logic that prevails in political states is diametrically opposed to that which prevails where God reigns (Rom 12:17-13:7). This does not eliminate the need for the state as the legitimate monopolizer of violence, but it does show that the essence of the Christian community is very different, and far more radical. The Christian churches have the function of showing to the whole world what that world can be when it places itself under the dominion of God. This function is difficult to fulfill when the churches assume, in "Constantinian" fashion, that they are no more than the religious dimension of society as a whole. Catholicism in the twentieth century has contemplated the collapse of all the last remnants of Christendom. Although many may still dream of a return to the past, the action of the Spirit appears to point in another direction. The century that saw the collapse of Christendom has also been the century of the birth of multiple forms of Christian community within the churches. In these humble beginnings, often despised by theology, are the seeds of a new, more hopeful Christianity, because its hope is not seen, although its first fruits are already being reaped. The maturing of a Christianity of communities, in unity and multiplicity, in spiritual richness and critical consciousness, is the great challenge of the new century. It is the gift that nourishes the hope of the churches.

7

The Trinitarian Reign of the Christian God

The reign of God proclaimed by Jesus and the first Christian community is a *trinitarian* reign. The word "Trinity," however, usually sounds quite strange to believers. It seems to suggest theological speculations that are removed from the daily practice of Christian communities and appropriate only for specialists. The question of the meaning of the Trinity for the life of the poor and for the transformation of the world may sound like a naive, if not impossible, attempt to unite opposite extremes: on the one hand, the practice of believers, and on the other, intricate metaphysical constructions that are derived from the history of Christian theology and that appear to lack all significance for actual praxis.

One effort to avoid these difficulties consists in proposing the Trinity as a model of community. This perspective demonstrates the relationship between the Trinity and the kingdom of God, and understands this kingdom as a highly meaningful project for the praxis of believers. In God himself, believers would find the model of what God desires to create in history: a loving community of free and equal persons. Nonetheless, it is not altogether clear that this linking of the kingdom of God and the Trinity is truly liberating. In some cases that may seem extreme, but are real in practice, it can lead both to converting the kingdom of God into a mere ideal, and to enclosing the Trinity in an immanence[1] separated from its acting in history. Let us examine this briefly.

THE TRINITY AS MODEL OF THE KINGDOM

If the Trinity is conceived primarily as a model of the kingdom of God, there follows a strong tendency to convert the kingdom of God into an *ideal* quite removed from our world. In our world the loving relationships proper to the Trinity simply do not prevail. Thus the kingdom of God would belong above all to the future. Certainly, Jesus not only preached the nearness of the reign of God, but also claimed that this reign was already present in the midst of the disciples (Mk 1:15; Lk 17:21). However, subsequent history would show that the promised kingdom was still not realized. Using Alfred Loisy's famous statement, though in a different sense, it could be said that "Jesus announced the kingdom of God; what came to be was the church."[2] Nonetheless, Christians would continue to be called to establish in the present time the kingdom that Jesus announced, by working for a more just and more human society.

From this point of view, the kingdom of God appears primarily as a *state of affairs*. It would mean a society free of poverty, injustice, inequality and violence; a society where there would be abundance, peace and fraternity. Thus, from this viewpoint, the Trinity would provide us with a model for relationships among human beings. It would be the paradigm on which we must base all our efforts to build a better world. It is important to note that in this perspective the Trinity acquires what was an ancient function of divinity in classical philosophy: it is the *Unmoved Mover* that attracts all things to itself, all things being moved ultimately by the desire to be like the Unmoved Mover. This does not discount the action of God's grace in history, but it emphasizes above all the paradigmatic character of the divine unity. As in Plato's conception, that unity is the paradigm that must inspire our efforts to build God's kingdom in history.

Thus, in this view of the kingdom and the Trinity, there is a tendency to emphasize *our ethical obligation to build the kingdom*, that is, to build a society that conforms to the model of social relations we find in the Trinity. God would be the ultimate support and the ground of our praxis. However, since God, having no hands or mouth or feet, does not act in our present-day history our praxis becomes the principal agent responsible for bringing the reign of God into history. That means, with respect to the Trinity, that *the actions of Jesus and of the Spirit tend to be separated from present history.* Jesus appears above all as the model of a praxis dedicated entirely to announcing and building the kingdom. In this sense, whether Jesus is or is not alive at the present time is not very relevant, because the decisive thing is that he shows us, *with his past life,* the way to struggle for a more just society in the present. In the same way, the function of the Holy Spirit in the present tends to be limited to inspiring our social struggles for the kingdom, even if it is not very clear what the difference is between general ethical obligations and the praxis more specific to believers, if indeed any difference exists.

This tendency to make God disappear as the subject of his reign necessarily involves the *appearance of other subjects destined to bring the reign about.* Obviously, these subjects will need to have sufficient power and influence to be able to do something significant in history. At times it was thought that the poor majorities could, of themselves, be the agents of their own liberation. Their impotence and their repeated failures, however, force one to consider other possible subjects, be they economic, social or political in nature. Indeed, the very church itself might become the principal subject of the realization of the reign of God, insofar as its leaders assume positions that influence and transform society. Such a theology of the kingdom can thus be adopted by both progressive and conservative theologians. In either case, it means an inevitable "immanentization" of the reality of the Trinity, removed from history. The salvific actions of the creator Father, of the redeemer Son and of the Spirit of love are presistently associated with the past history of salvation, while the present is handed over to other subjects. Thus the only Trinity relevant for the present is the one which, removed from history into pure transcendent immanence, serves as the model for the city that we are striving to build.

From the viewpoint of the poor, this conception of the relationship between the Trinity and the kingdom of God *is not especially hopeful.* The poor are less capable of transforming history than other more powerful subjects, so that their historical function tends to become subsidiary. Their role is limited to supporting the works that others do to advance the future kingdom of God, in which all inequality will disappear. Meanwhile, though, the inequality continues, even in relation to their future liberators. Moreover, the already oppressive life of the poor is loaded down with one further obligation: in addition to assuring their own survival, they are also required to support the efforts of other subjects to transform society. In any case, the poor are converted into mere recipients of a future kingdom, without being able to consider themselves already true citizens of that kingdom. Their hope has no pledges or first fruits (Rom 8:23; 2 Cor 5:5). Moreover, in this conception the Trinity itself serves as a rather abstract model that seems hardly significant for present historical praxis. In fact, it is not even very clear why we must speak precisely of a *trinity*: four, or six, or ninety divine persons could just as well serve as a model for community.

Obviously this summary sketch does not claim to describe any concrete theology, but rather to show the extreme tendencies of a conception of the Trinity which, although it seeks to serve as an inspiration for a liberating praxis, does not always turn out to be especially useful for such praxis. Does this mean, then, that the Trinity must remain a purely metaphysical speculation? Or are there other conceptions of the Trinity that are more relevant for the life of the poor and the transformation of the world?

THE TRINITARIAN REIGN OF GOD

We will try to sketch now an idea of the Trinity that can be truly relevant and liberating with regard to our present praxis. It takes as a premise that the Trinity acts today in our history, and its action is precisely that of reigning. The reign of God is indissolubly united to the Trinity, not because the Trinity is a model, but because the Trinity expresses our experience of a God who in fact reigns in history, as true as it may be that the reign has not yet reached its culmination.

The Dynamism of the Spirit

Our language about the Trinity does not derive from abstract considerations that we must subsequently re-work in order to make relevant for the present. Nor does it simply enunciate ideals for the future. Discourse about the Trinity *derives from the concrete Christian experience of liberation in the present.* It is a way of speaking about God that is indissolubly linked to an experience: the present experience of the *Spirit.* This experience can have a quite varied phenomenology, including personal and collective experiences such as pardon, reconciliation, bodily and spiritual health, or the beginning of a renewed life in community. Obviously, this experience of the Spirit is a valid Christian experience only when enthusiasm in the Spirit does not lead to forgetting the cross of the Son (2 Cor 13:2-4), and when the newness of an unexpected fraternity with other believers does not degenerate into separatist isolationism. The perfect community is one that, like the Father himself, remains universally open to the just and to sinners (Mt 5:44-48). Expressed in other terms, the Christian experience of the Spirit is authentic only when it is already, here and now, a trinitarian experience.

From this point of view, the reign of God is not primarily a state of affairs, but *a dynamism* that is already present in history, subverting it from below. The reign of God is the fact that God reigns. It is therefore a reign before it is a kingdom. The kingdom, understood as diverse possible states of affairs in history, will rather be the consequence of God's actual reigning. The essential thing, therefore, is a dynamism, and this dynamism has two terms. On the one hand, there are those aspects and dimensions of the world that in fact oppose the reign of God, over which God still cannot reign. They are the economic, political, social and religious powers that oppose God's designs for history, and which, for that reason, are ultimately responsible for injustice, suffering and oppression. The other term is made up of those realms of creation over which God is indeed able to exercise his reign. This means, very concretely, that in these realms every form of domination of some human beings over others disappears, because where God in fact reigns there are no other kings or lords. It is not a question, properly speaking, of a theocracy, for the Christian God desires to share his reign with the citizens thereof (2 Tim 2:12).

This dynamism, therefore, has the character of *an exodus.* The reign of the trinitarian God is the same reign of God that Moses proclaims after the liberation from slavery in Egypt. And like every exodus, the reign of God requires a people. There is no reign if there is no people to reign over. This does not mean that there do not exist in creation many realms over which God exercises his reign, even if there is no explicit consciousness of such. Where there is love, God is there. Nevertheless, the mystery of God's plan for history requires the existence of a people over whom God's reign becomes explicit, so that it can be proclaimed clearly to all humanity what actually happens when God reigns. And what happens is precisely this: God's reign creates, starting now and from below, reconciled communities of brothers and sisters in which inequality, poverty and domination no longer exist. More radically, they are communities from which have disappeared the useless fear of God, the insatiable desire for power, and the radical serpentine pretension to justify ourselves by the results of our own praxis.[3]

The Work of Christ

From the Christian viewpoint, such liberation can happen only as the work of a God who is both one and triune. However much this liberation might occur in our praxis, transform our praxis, and enliven and inspire our praxis, this liberation is ultimately *a work of the triune God*, who in this way affirms and realizes his reign over our historical praxis. The power to free us belongs only to God, and not to any of the many chieftains of the world (Ps 108:12). What must be explained, then, is why precisely it is a *triune* God who frees us.

In the eyes of the Christian faith, the life, death and resurrection of Christ have a central function in our liberation. This is what classical theology calls the "work of Christ." In what does this work consist? In his life, Christ proclaimed the poor to be the privileged recipients of God's love. This proclamation obviously breaks with the Adamic pretension of self-justification, which is the ultimate root of human sin. Those who wish to live from the fruits of their actions proclaim their successes as the deserved results of their own efforts. This means, conversely, that all the wretched people of history are doing no more than reaping the corresponding results of their own faults.[4] In the same way, the Adamic pretension of self-justification leads us to use other people, the environment and even our very selves as means to augment our own power to produce the results that will justify us. Thus arise domination, the lust for power and prestige, and the destruction of the natural environment. Jesus of Nazareth, by contrast, announces a God who is a good Father, who makes the sun to shine on the just and on sinners (Mt 5:45) and who recompenses all equally, independently of their merits. For that reason Jesus is perceived as a blasphemer, and as a threat to the religious, social and political powers that are founded ultimately on the Adamic logic of merits.

This confrontation culminates *on the cross*. There Jesus undergoes the fate of all the victims of history. His death is interpreted by that same logic as the deserved punishment for his impiety and rebelliousness. God does not in fact intervene to save him from death; thus, from the viewpoint of his executioners, the non-intervention of God confirms Jesus' guilt. But a divine rescue of Jesus, although it would have affirmed his justness, would also have confirmed the presumed culpability of all the poor, sick and marginalized people in history who have been seen as abandoned by God. God does not intervene, and Christ experiences abandonment by God. However, Christian faith affirms, with the centurion at the cross, that Christ was the Son of God (Mk 15:39). That is, Christian faith asserts that God, in Christ, was reconciling the world with himself (2 Cor 5:19). All the fundamental affirmations of the Christian faith, including the Christian conception of God as one and triune, emerge from this interpretation of the cross: *crux probat omnia*. If God was in Christ, that means, on the one hand, that God has experienced in himself the fate of the poor, the sick, the marginalized, indeed the fate of all the victims of history. The one who was to serve as the guarantor of a correspondence between our actions and their results has borne the presumed consequences of all offenses. But if God was in Christ on the cross, that also means that God has not intervened to save the just and to punish the sinners. Rather, God has annulled the schema of the law by personally bearing its ultimate consequences. In this way God made possible the pardon and the reconciliation of the whole of humankind.

This cannot be anything else but a trinitarian event: God himself, in Christ, has experienced abandonment by God. The expression, "My God, my God, why have you forsaken me?" (Mk 15:34) does not refer, as has often been said, to the humanity of Christ as opposed to his divinity (or, as Hilary of Poitiers said, to the humanity that saw itself abandoned by the divinity). The abandonment refers to God himself, who personally experiences God's remoteness, the reality of death and what theology has classically called "the descent into hell." This is the situation of those who have been presumably abandoned by God all through history. This abandonment of God by God can only be expressed, given the limits of our language, as a difference between God and God. It is not a question, as Moltmann would have it, of a confrontation or a division in the divinity.[5] It is a question of God's personally experiencing in Christ, without ceasing to be God, the fate of those who appear to be abandoned by God in history. And God suffers this fate in a real way, not as a farce: the God who is called upon does not come, and Christ is not saved from the cross. This experience of abandonment, however, is not a rupture in the divinity, for on the cross it is the one and only God who personally suffers the fate of Christ. God is not only the Son who assumes the fate of all the victims of history and the punishments presumably destined for sinners. On the cross God continues to be the good Father who makes the sun to shine on the just and on sinners. Only in this way can God justify all the victims, while at the same time making possible a historical way toward reconciliation.

The abandonment of God by God is in fact the beginning of reconciliation only if it is not interpreted as a metaphysical division within the divinity. The existence of two gods, one acting in solidarity with the victims and another pardoning the executioners, would not be capable of breaking down the wall of division between the two groups. The abandonment of God by God, if it were a rupture in the divinity, would mean a divinization of suffering, in the way that occasionally happens in the history of religions. The abandonment of God by God is truly liberating precisely because there is no rupture in the divinity. There continues to be a bond of union between the Father and the Son. And this bond of union is precisely the Spirit. The identification of God with Christ not only means that God personally experiences abandonment by God. The identification of God with Christ also means that death has no power over Christ (Acts 4:24). If God has identified completely with Christ, death no longer can dominate him (Rom 6:9). Stated in other terms: Christ is alive; he has risen from the dead. The resurrection shows us that the abandonment suffered by the Son is not a rupture in the divinity. Although God did not make himself present by saving Christ from the cross, God was always present because the bond of union between the Father and the Son was never broken. The identification of God with Christ is possible because the real difference between the Father and the Son is not a rupture, but a bond of love that we call the Spirit. For that reason we should not find it strange that Paul expressly tells us that the Spirit raised Jesus from the dead (Rom 8:11).

The Relation with the Father

In this way, then, it becomes clear that the work of Christ can be fully understood only as a trinitarian work. Only if God is Father, Son and Spirit is our reconciliation possible. And only if these real differences in God do not signify a tritheist division in the divinity can the Adamic logic of self-justification lose its power over us. That loss of power can be explained only by the presence of the Spirit in history, blowing where she will. Indeed, the abolition of the human pretension of self-justification is possible only *through faith*. This is not an arbitrary matter. Christian faith is precisely the confidence that God himself, on the cross of Christ, has annulled the schema of correspondence between our actions and their results. This means, at one and the same time, the pardon of sinners (who do not receive their punishment) and the justification of the poor (who are freed from their presumed culpability and their presumed abandonment by God). To the extent that we believe in that work of God in Christ, to the same extent are we freed from the pretension of justifying ourselves and from the culpability which declares us to be deserving of our misfortunes.

Of course, Christian faith cannot be conceived as a new kind of merit on our part. If that were so, we ourselves would be the authors of our own justification, and we would not have escaped the logic of Adam. Faith can only be a gift of God. It is God's work in us. More concretely: it is the work of the Spirit. "No one can say 'Jesus is Lord' except by the Spirit" (1 Cor 12:3). This is of crucial importance because it shows us the trinitarian meaning of faith. By faith we know that Christ has borne the punishments that presumably correspond to our sins. We no longer need expiatory sacrifices, because Christ's death is the sacrifice that does away with the internal logic of all sacrifices. By faith we also know that Christ has identified with the poor, the marginalized, the vanquished and the sick, thus showing them his love and freeing them from the culpability that declares their situation to be deserved. In this way, by faith we are reconciled with God, whom we can call *Abba, Father*. In other words, by faith we can participate in the relationship of the Son with the Father. And this is made possible precisely by the Spirit who inspires our faith. So does Paul express it: "For you did not receive a spirit that makes you a slave again to fear, but you received the Spirit of sonship. And by him we cry 'Abba, Father' " (Rom 8:15; Gal 4:6).

Our liberation from the old logic is heavy with consequences. First and foremost, through it Christ is experienced as a living person, capable of realizing in our personal and community life that which he realized once and for all on the cross. If the logic of Adam produces idols and lords who would guarantee correspondence between our actions and their fruits, all that is reversed in the logic of Christ. The disciples of Christ no longer have idols or fathers or kings or lords or teachers (Mt 23:1-12). Over them reigns only Christ himself, who is now the one who exercises the reign in the name of the Father. The identification of God with Christ not only implies his resurrection, but also his exaltation at the right hand of the throne of God (Heb 8:1; 12:2), where he has been constituted as *Lord*. This throne is no heavenly seat, but the symbol of the reign of God, which is now exercised by Christ. In the measure that this reign is made possible by the Spirit who raised Christ and who also raises us up from sin, it can also be said that "the Lord is the Spirit" (2 Cor 3:17). This reign is not a spiritual entity, but a reality in history. God reigns wherever, by faith, the consequences of Adam's sin disappear and a reconciled community appears, one in which goods are shared, social differences fade away and poverty is overcome.

This presents a challenge to the powers of this world, not only because of the appearance of an alternative form of life, but because the reign of Jesus as Messiah in the present time stands in contradiction to every other form of sovereignty present in history (Acts 17:7). The redemption wrought by Christ is not purely individual or spiritual, but involves a transformation of all the relationships of power in history. Put in biblical terms: God "canceled the written code, with its regulations, that was against us, and that stood opposed to us; he took it away, nailing it to the cross. And having disarmed the powers and the authorities, he made a public spectacle of them, triumphing over them by the cross" (Col 2:14-15). In reality, the reign of Jesus means that all other reigns belong to a vanishing epoch and, although they may perform a historical function where the Adamic schema of deserts still prevails, they are doomed to disappear when the reign of Christ reaches its fullness and is finally returned to the Father. Then all injustice and all domination will have disappeared from history, and God will be all in all (1 Cor 15:23-24).

CONCLUSION

The reign of God, therefore, is not a utopia for the future, but a dynamism that is already acting in history. The reign is already present there where Jesus reigns, in the community of his disciples. This community, however, is not the reign of God. The reign of God is the dynamic exercise of God's sovereignty in creation and in history, exercised by the Son through the Spirit. This Spirit, although it blows where it will, becomes explicitly present there where believers can call God "Father" without fear, forming fraternal communities of brothers and sisters. The other struggles and efforts to transform history continue to be as urgent and necessary as before. It is in the Christian communities, however, that the most subversive and radical transformation begins to occur, because in them the power of Adam's sin has disappeared and, with it, all the consequent forms of dependency, oppression and death. Of course, this transformation of history is possible only in a trinitarian form. God is the one who liberates us, and that liberation has a strictly trinitarian character. Only in the abandonment of God by God, in the newness of faith, and in *our* inclusion, by the Spirit, in the relationship of God with God, is a radical transformation of history possible.

From this point of view it also becomes obvious that the Trinity is not primarily an abstract model of community. More than a model, the Trinity is the concrete form in which our God brings about a community that is not *our* community, but *God's* own community, the community between the Father and the Son by work of the Spirit. The Spirit, by including us through faith in the relationship between the Son and the Father, does not provide us with a model, but incorporates us into the very life of the Trinity, thus radically transforming human history, from this moment and from below. For this reason, any modalist conception of the Trinity is devoid of a liberative perspective, since the Trinity is not only the "mode" in which God reveals himself *ad extra* in the history of salvation. Precisely because the Trinity expresses analogously the very reality of God, our participation in the relationship of Christ with God is nothing less than inclusion in the divine life itself. The communities that God creates in history are not the realm of a merely external reign. They are the realm where God's trinitarian life itself becomes embodied in history. Salvation is not only sanctification as a separation from or alternative to the world. Salvation is inclusion in trinitarian life. Then indeed there is something new in history.

From this point of view, the Trinity expresses a real hope for the poor, and above all for the poor with Spirit, for theirs is the reign of God. God continually surprises the wise and the prudent of this world, creating communities among the poor in which they emerge from their desperation and their culpability and are made into free managers of their own lives. In these communities the first fruits of a new world are experienced; poverty, inequality and injustice begin to be surmounted, from this moment and from below. These poor people realize that it will not be other benefactors who transform the world on their behalf, but it is God in person who, starting now, has begun this transformation. For that reason they themselves take up the word and "speak in tongues" without needing others to speak in their name. For the poor without Spirit, the Christian communities constitute a visible sign, right now, of what God desires to do with the poor of the earth, which is nothing other than to free them from poverty, from domination and from every form of dependency, whether explicit or veiled.

This hope, however, is not only for the poor, but for everyone.

The executioners and the sinners receive the announcement of the pardon of their sins, and the invitation to join a new fraternity. The rich and the powerful receive the concrete possibility of renouncing their wealth and their power, in order to become part of the new reality that God creates in history. What is expected of them is not primarily great charitable or political works. What is expected of them, more radically, is that, leaving behind familial and material bonds, they come to form part, as equals, as brothers and sisters, of those communities in which God makes his trinitarian reign present in history. Obviously, all this is impossible without work and without human effort. Nonetheless, the ultimate initiative that makes every renunciation possible is none other than God's initiative, which enables us, through the Spirit, to place our confidence in him. Only thus can we collaborate with God in the exercise of his reign. In this way there opens up for all humanity the possibility of a radical transformation of history, a transformation in which all are invited to become part of the fraternal banquet, our feeble analogy for God's trinitarian life itself.

8

Theology's Past and Liberation's Future

A full accounting of liberation theology will possibly require both greater historical distance than we now have from it, and a space more extensive than the present work allows. Still, critical reflection on the path traversed thus far by liberation theology is an urgent task for those of us who believe that many of its great intuitions are necessary for the future of all Christian theology. The future, however, can never consist in a simple repetition of the past. When that happens, dogmatism only tries, unsuccessfully, to conceal despair. Let us try then to view our past without dogmatism, seeking thus to leave open a door to that hope which comes directly from the gospel itself (Col 1:23).

A NEW THEOLOGY

Liberation theology undoubtedly has a variety of roots, including the Second Vatican Council in the Catholic church, the political movements for national liberation in the so-called "third world," the contemporary European theology in which many Latin American theologians were trained, and the different pastoral experiences that gave rise to the base communities. There is, however, one major event that turns out to be an even more important and decisive factor than these others: the discovery of the social situation in Latin America as a challenge to Christian faith. The poverty of millions of persons and the enormous inequalities between rich and poor in a presumably "Christian" continent were the principal incentives for reflection about the practical dimen-

160

sions and consequences of faith. Obviously this major event continues to confront us today, challenging all theology. No intellectual fashion can conceal it.

Liberation theology had two great intuitions, which I continue to consider theologically valid: the so-called "perspective of the poor" and the "primacy of praxis." From these intuitions there arose a new Christology, interested in showing, as had never been done up to that point, the theological relevance of Jesus' practice of solidarity with the poorest people. Several christological themes then took on a decisive importance:

1) Above all, liberation theology emphasized Jesus' involvement in the world of the poor, just as this involvement appears in the scriptures. It was an involvement that not only evinced the general solidarity with the human race that took place in the incarnation, but one that introduced into the world of the poor a transforming dynamism that aimed at a complete renewal of their reality. Christian salvation, from this point of view, could no longer be considered a purely spiritual process or simply an other-worldly fulfillment. Christian salvation, from the biblical viewpoint, includes essentially (and not just as a further consequence) a genuine transformation of social relationships now, and in this world. This perspective made possible new and fresh readings of the Bible.

2) Second, liberation theology emphasized that Jesus' preaching was radically linked to the announcement of the imminent arrival of the reign of God. This was, of course, something that European exegesis had already pointed out much earlier. Jesus' announcement of God's reign, however, had represented for some theologians a serious problem, for evidently that reign had not arrived with the immediacy that Jesus had proclaimed. Liberation theology was able to take up that theme again and point out the social dimensions of God's reign. In this way the growth of liberation movements in Latin America made the imminence of God's reign, with all its social consequences, less of a theological problem: the reign announced by Jesus appeared on the verge of arriving.

3) Another christological dimension also came to the forefront. The practice and the message of Jesus brought him into conflict with the authorities of his time. In contrast to the traditional sentimental images of Jesus, liberation theology emphasized that Jesus'

solidarity with the poor and his announcement of God's reign implied an inevitable clash with the most powerful. Such was surely the experience of many Christians, who began to pay a high price, often paying with their very lives, for the new pastoral orientations that liberation theology inspired.

Indeed, all these christological discoveries pointed to a new conception of the following and the imitation of Jesus. To follow Jesus meant a new way of loving: Christian love, in imitation of Jesus' love, has a constitutively social dimension. Or, as it was then the custom to say, Christian love is a "political love," which has to shape the entire task of the Christian church. The new theology urged church leaders to support the political movements that were fighting for social change, with variations that went from reform to revolution. Of course, all this had enormous consequences for a "Catholic" continent. Catholicism was then the confession of almost all Latin Americans. If the authority and the power of the Catholic church were put on the side of social transformation, many changes would take place in Latin America. If such a powerful church "opted for the poor," an unrestrainable tide would be let loose. Naturally, Rome and Washington soon took notice of this.

ANALYZING THE CRISIS

After the boon of the seventies and eighties, it is difficult to avoid speaking of a crisis in liberation theology. The important thing, in my view, is not to deny the facts, but to try to analyze them and learn from them. Let us try then to consider several elements of the crisis.

1) One element that is perhaps superficial, but not irrelevant, is the partial defeat and the transformation of the national liberation movements at the end of the twentieth century. To be sure, liberation theology was not simply an ideological spokesperson for those movements. But neither was it foreign to them. In great measure, liberation theology related its practice to and placed its concrete hopes in the success of these movements. It is clear that the massive poverty and the inequalities to which these movements tried to respond have not disappeared. It is also clear that the

national liberation movements were defeated by the brutal reaction of local oligarchies and the central imperial power. All the same, I believe we already have sufficient distance from them so as to realize the profound strategic limits of such movements and to learn from the experience. It does not appear very wise to try to transform at a merely national level an economic system—capitalism—that is clearly global. In any case, the current examples of resistance to injustice appear now to be taking other routes, which do not involve the seizure of power in a national state. When the resistance does seize power, it appears to have no other options than a light social-democracy or the most disgraceful populism.

2) Another element of the crisis concerns the reaction that took place within the Catholic church. Clearly, Catholic leaders did not give massive support to the new theological tendencies, and from the start there was a profound conflict among the clergy. In this division, the Vatican curia clearly sided with the conservative sector, as was shown in the systematic naming of bishops who were decidedly opposed to liberation theology. The leaders who most favored liberation theology were marginalized in not very subtle ways. In many cases, there was close collaboration among the ecclesiastical hierarchy, local oligarchies, military groups and the U.S. administration. Even the assassination of Catholic leaders favorable to liberation theology was accepted with a certain acquiescence ("they were involved in politics") by conservative Catholics. A new Catholic clergy, trained in a profound theological and political conservatism, has been steadily assuming positions in the ecclesiastical chain of command and will have a powerful influence on the future of Catholicism in Latin America.

3) If the elements of the crisis were limited to the two pointed out so far, it would be easy to cast the blame on Washington and Rome, and thus avoid any self-criticism. The sins of Moscow and Havana could perhaps also be added in, but theology itself would have nothing basically new to discover. There is another element of the crisis, however, which has to do with the "major event" that grounds liberation theology. It is not that there have ceased to be poor people, but that poor people seem not to have opted for liberation theology. A Guatemalan Catholic religious sister with much grassroots experience stated it this way: "The Catholic church opted for the poor, but the poor opted for Pentecostalism." The

expression might be simple, but it contains a great truth. The poor of Latin America are no longer massively Catholic. We are not talking only about the increase in Pentecostal-type Protestant churches. Many Latin Americans, especially in the poor urban sectors, now do not belong to any Christian church, or are far removed from any habitual practice of religion. Although this is not a European-style secularization, there is no doubt that an important cultural change is taking place in Latin America. In any case, in countries where liberation theology had an important popular response, its influence has declined quite considerably. The base communities have declined significantly and in some cases have been transformed into non-governmental development organizations, thus losing their popular base.

It is possible to blame Washington and say that "the sects" (as many Catholics still call the free churches) are the result of an imperialist conspiracy. Such a claim can doubtless explain some isolated facts at a given historical moment, but not the extraordinary growth of a movement which by definition lacks a centralized administration. Why do the poor become Pentecostals? Why within the Catholic church do the movements of a charismatic nature flourish? Why, even in poor parishes run by liberation-theology-minded priests, do the charismatic movements constitute the majority of the active membership? No doubt the old theme of the "opium of the people" can be taken out and dusted off, and it can be said that the poor people who belong to these Pentecostal and charismatic movements are alienated, naive, easily fooled, in search of consolation and escape, etc. This can explain some of the phenomena, but is it the whole truth? Above all, are those who make these claims being true to the fundamental intuitions of liberation theology?

Let us recall that one of the fundamental intuitions of this theology was precisely the "perspective of the poor." Liberation theology stated that poor people are in a privileged situation for truly understanding the gospel. For that very reason, the gospel of Jesus and of the first communities had been directed primarily to the poor. Theology, it was said, had to learn from the poor. Theology, it was said, is the second act, while Christian practice, especially that of the poor, is the first act. When poor people do not act the way that that theology foresaw, is the question to be resolved simply by declaring them alienated and ignorant? Or is it necessary to revise the theology critically? This is an important dilemma, *because it is precisely fidelity to one of the principles of liberation theology that seems inevitably to lead us beyond that theology*, at least beyond its classic forms. We are dealing with fidelity not only to a theological principle, but to a principle that seems to be clearly anchored in the testimony of the gospel. It concerns fidelity to and respect for the poor themselves and their religious experience. Instead of seeking to be "the voice of the voiceless," does it not make more sense to listen to the voices of the poor and their churches, even when those voices sound strident to the cultivated, half-European ears of the theologians?

RETURNING TO THE GOSPEL

If we opt for a critical revision of liberation theology with an eye to the future, we must return to the gospel, not to engage in conservative criticism of the limits and the lacunae in liberation theology, but to supersede those limits and fill in those lacunae. Only thus will the liberation that comes from Jesus' practice and preaching have a future. In this sense, the problem is not, and never can be, in liberation theology's christological and evangelical emphasis. It is rather in the fact that this emphasis was not sufficiently radical. Let us examine this briefly.

1) Liberation theology was correct in pointing out that solidarity with the poor was one of the fundamental dimensions of Jesus' praxis. However, it is not enough to say *what* it was that Jesus did; it is necessary to know also *how* Jesus did it. Jesus' closeness to the poor and the transformation that he brought about in their lives had an essential dimension that has not always received sufficient emphasis. Jesus called the poor *to faith*. Jesus asked of his generation an unconditional adherence to his person, without which the transformations proper to the messianic era were impossible. The changes that occurred in the lives of the poor, the sick and the outcast could not be explained without faith: "your faith has saved you," repeats Jesus before the radical liberations that his presence produces among the poor. Only a brutal exegetical surgery allows the amputation of this call to a personal and liberating faith from

the praxis of Jesus, in order to attribute it to Paul or some other strata of the New Testament.

2) The central theme of the preaching of Jesus was undoubtedly the reign of God. It is important, though, to point out that the reign of God was for Jesus something more than a social utopia. The social transformations proper to God's reign are those which God introduces right there where God himself reigns, displacing other rulers. The background of the Exodus and the Mosaic law itself, with all its measures in favor of the poor, provided the paradigm for understanding what happens when God himself, and not the Pharaoh, rules (Ex 15:18). The introduction of other monarchs in Israel, understood by the Old Testament both as treason toward God and as the origin of injustice and idolatry, provided at the same time a hope for the coming of a future king anointed to govern in justice: a Messiah. More radically, though, it introduced the hope that God himself, in person, would come again to govern his people, freeing them from the oppression of false rulers (Ez 34). The announcement of God's reign was, for Jesus, the announcement that the time was fulfilled and God himself was coming to take charge of his people.

Jesus' call to faith is, in this respect, inseparable from his proclamation of the reign of God. By faith people accept God's sovereignty over their lives, and become free from the rule of every other power. Faith not only allows miracles, but undermines the rule of Satan and makes possible the irruption of God's reign. Jesus obviously believed that all of Israel was called to accept the direct sovereignty of God, thus becoming that alternative society destined to attract all nations to a final pilgrimage that would transform the history of humanity. Israel's progressive rejection of this call obliged Jesus to concentrate his work on a small community, one characterized by faith and destined to establish itself as a representation in miniature of what Israel was called to be. Thus is explained the symbolic choice of the twelve representatives of the tribes of Israel. It was a renewed Israel governed by a new law, as expressed in the Sermon on the Mount; an Israel characterized by faith and therefore prepared to make possible the incorporation of the Gentile nations. Thus would a new people be formed, over whom God could rule once more (Mt 8:10-12).

3) Certainly Jesus entered into conflict with the powerful. He

did so not just by criticizing their injustices. Much more radically, his announcement of the imminent arrival of God's reign placed in question not only the sovereignty of the Roman occupiers, but also the sovereignty of Israel's own rulers. God himself was going to take direct charge of his people. Rendering to God what was God's and rendering to Caesar what was Caesar's meant economic independence (getting rid of all the denarii) and socio-political transformation: the usurping tenants would have to return the people to their rightful owner. The radicality of Jesus' aspirations made conflict inevitable.

Nonetheless, Jesus instructed his disciples, his "little flock" (Lk 12:32) of followers, concerning original ways to deal with conflict. Over against the logic of the powerful, based on the idea of retribution, Jesus proposes not responding to the wicked with the same evil that they cause, but rather confusing them with innovative strategies that bewilder the oppressors and challenge their way of acting (Mt 5:38-48). Jesus' non-violence does not arise from concern for "the sacredness of life" or other general ethical considerations. His non-violence is a concrete strategy for resisting oppression, one that seeks to eliminate the basis of oppression at its root. By contrast, those who overcome oppressors by using the oppressors' own means *must have as much power to do damage as the oppressors themselves,* and they end up being very similar to those over whom they have triumphed. What nation stands out today for its militarism and for its lack of respect for international law more conspicuously than that country—the United States—that contributed decisively to the military defeat of Hitler? Who else but the state of Israel has put into practice the shameful annexation of foreign territories by reason of new versions of the Nazi doctrine of "vital space"? Human history has many other examples of what Jesus sought to avoid for the people over whom God would reign.

All this gives to Jesus' liberating practice an absolutely original style, which is difficult to reconcile with many traditional ecclesiastical practices. There is no need to seize power in order to realize social changes from above. The Messiah, the anointed king, renounced being king over Israel (Jn 6:15) and confronted his enemies unarmed. Jesus prefers to begin in the present and to begin from below: to begin from below a transformation that touches the basic structures of the system and challenges the system in its totality. The church should not think of penetrating into the palaces and the power centers with the aim of instructing rulers about how to conduct their affairs ethically. Nor is it adequate to change an alliance with today's power-brokers for an alliance with those who seek to be powerful tomorrow. What is needed is that the Christian communities be placed effectively under the rule of the Messiah, which is—for those who confess the divinity of Jesus Christ—the very reign of God. To the degree that such communities exist, the social utopia of the future becomes a reality of the present. Social differences disappear, and poor people take their seat upon the thrones of the kingdom. Only in this way does a historically visible praxis arise that can question what the princes of this world do with authority (and not by virtue of an empty invocation of the law, such as that of the scribes and the Pharisees).

It is interesting to observe that the Latin American poor seem to have found in diverse Pentecostal and charismatic movements *some of the characteristics that liberation theology—and Catholicism in general—seems to have lacked historically.* First of all, the poor have found in these movements a call to personal faith, which is bound to challenge seriously the idea of a "Christian continent." Such an idea is defensible only if faith is reduced to its cultural and folkloric elements, and no account is taken of the absolutely personal and gratuitous moment of encounter with God. Second, and in contrast to certain stereotypes about "Protestant individualism," this personal faith inserts the believers into a community of disciples in which concrete forms of acceptance and solidarity are found. Indeed, this faith proclaims the real existence of a God and a risen Messiah who rules directly over his people. Such faith significantly reduces the number and hierarchy of sacred mediators and reduces to a secondary level those powerful ones (present or future, conservative or revolutionary) who were traditionally thought to be the historical channels of God's saving will. In this way God's here-and-now reign brings with it a social and economic transformation that begins already in the present, and out of the concrete life of the poor (fraternity, healings, economic betterment), without having to wait for some uncertain future in which rulers will behave more ethically or be replaced by more acceptable alternatives. The poor were not so mistaken or alienated after all: the Spirit of God seems still to be preferring them today.

Latin American Protestantism, however, has hardly suffered persecution from the powerful. The reason is that the real transformations that are taking place among the poor are not being articulated by a theology with a general vision of the social change required by faith. When Latin American Pentecostals have tried to think about social change, they have often vacillated within coordinates like those of Constantinian Catholicism. Or they have believed that social change is the mere consequence of the individual change of each person, so that the increase in conversions will automatically bring on the social revolution. Or they have thought that social change will be achieved when honest and authentic politicians (preferably Christian) take control in the presidential palaces, using, of course, the coercive power and the violence that are intrinsic to every state. Thus they lose sight of the structural, radical and concrete way that scripture understands social change, including the function that the believing community has in this structural change, insofar as it is already the visible beginning of the new eon. What is even more serious, they lose sight of what the Spirit herself is doing in the churches wherein the poor experience an authentic social and economic transformation of their lives. The structural change from below is replaced by reforms or false revolutions from above. It seems that in the last sixteen centuries the enemy has not had to be especially original when it comes to tempting the churches politically. He has only had to repeat the temptations he proposed to Jesus.

All the same, the enemy is defeated and falls like lightning wherever the gospel has begun to free humanity from the Adamic logic of self-justification and deserts, wherever new persons and new social relationships are made possible by faith. The liberation that Jesus came to effect has a future in this humanity that is so divided by fear, injustice, selfishness and religious ties. The fundamental intuitions of liberation theology can be reformulated for a theology in keeping with our times, a theology that can account for what the Spirit is already realizing by faith in the popular Christian movements. Such a theology will have a radical, biblical vision of social change: it will be social change that is initiated from below and that questions the paternalism and verticalism of the established churches. It will be social change that confronts every established power with the new authority of God's reign that is already visible in history, already visible in the communities of equals wherein all reign with Jesus, and wherein there is born a democratic sensibility capable of restoring the values of our presently ailing societies. Such communities will practice—from below and starting right now—new forms of economic solidarity, on the basis of which it will be possible to challenge the powerful, and without which there will be nobody capable of bringing about social change. Such a challenge to power, though, knows that not all have faith (1 Th 3:2) and therefore requires an essential tolerance and pluralism. Still, it will be an effective challenge, because it brings about what it preaches and preaches that which it has seen with its own eyes. It is the radical effectiveness of those who by God's grace are willing to return good for evil, washing their own clothes in the blood of the Lamb, for they believe that only thus will a way to liberation be opened that no Babylon in our history will be able to close. It will be a liberation that can say from this very moment, with modesty and gratitude: come and you will see: thus is our Messiah; thus is his reign; thus is the future of humanity.

Notes

2. The Gospel of Faith and Justice

[1]I will not tire the reader with bibliographic references. The researcher who needs them may find them in my study entitled *Teología de la praxis evangélica* (Santander, 1999). The specialist will not fail to notice in this text the presence of the work of exegetes and biblical theologians such as N. Lohfink, J. H. Yoder, J. Driver, R. Pesch, J. Mateos and G. Lohfink.

3. Matthew 25 and the Hope of the Poor

[1]Cf. I. Ellacuría, "La teología como momento ideológico de la praxis eclesial," *Estudios eclesiásticos* 53 (1978), 457-476.

[2]Cf. X. Pikaza, *Hermanos de Jesús y servidores de los más pequeños* (Mt 25:31-46) (Salamanca, 1984), pp. 300-302.

[3]Cf. N. Lohfink, *La opción por los pobres* (México, 1998), pp. 68-72.

[4]This last opinion is that of W. Trilling, *El verdadero Israel. La teología de Mateo* (Madrid, 1974), pp. 37-39.

[5]Cf. J.-V. Ingelaere, "La 'parabole' du jugement dernier (Matthieu 25:31-46)," in *Revue d'Histoire et de Philosophie Religieuses* 50 (1970) 23-60.

[6]Cf. J. Jeremias, *Las parábolas de Jesús* (Estella, 1997), p. 233.

[7]See a recent book of W. Cesar and R. Shaull on *Pentecostalismo e futuro das igrejas cristãs* (Petrópolis, 1999). My review of the book appears as chapter five of this book.

[8]A general vision of the meaning of the "option for the poor" in liberation theology can be found in G. Gutiérrez, "Pobres y opción fundamental," in I. Ellacuría and J. Sobrino, *Mysterium liberationis*, vol. I (Madrid, 1990), pp. 303-322. (ET: *Mysterium Libarationis* [Orbis Books, 1993], pp. 235-250.) On the Catholic ecclesial problem, see J. M. Castillo, *Escuchar lo que dicen los pobres a la iglesia* (Barcelona, 1999).

[9]Cf. González, *Teología de la praxis evangélica*, pp. 273-327.

[10]See concrete references in González, *Teología de la praxis evangélica*, pp. 127-173. Regarding the *generalizing* consideration of religions as

"human efforts to reach God apart from faith" (Kraemer) or as "ways of salvation desired by God" (Dupuis), I believe that Christian theology requires an internal analysis of each one of them, in order to see in what sense each of the religions, in each of their complex moments, is salvific or oppressive. The religious dialogue must do justice to the tremendous plurality of religions.

[11]J. Moltmann states something similar in his *Experiences in Theology. Ways and Forms of Christian Theology* (London: SCM Press, 2000), p. 237.

[12]Cf. E. Lohse, *Introducción al Nuevo Testamento* (Madrid, 1975), pp. 150-158.

[13]Cf. E.W. Stegemann and W. Stegemann, *Urchristliche Sozialgeschichte. Die Anfänge im Judentum und die Christusgemeinden in der mediterranen Welt* (Stuttgart, 1995). They base themselves on the opinion of M. D. Goulder, *Midrash and Lection in Matthew* (London: SPCK, 1974); Künzel, *Studien zum Gemeindeverständnis des Mattäusevangeliums* (Stuttgart, 1978), p. 251; F. W. Beare, *The Gospel According to Matthew. A Commentary* (New York: Harper & Row, 1982); J. A. Overman, *Matthew's Gospel and Formative Judaism. The Social World of the Matthean Community* (Minneapolis: Fortress, 1990).

[14]Cf. for *doûlos*: Mt 8:9; 10:24f; 13:27; 18:23,26-28,32; 20:27; 21:34ff; 24:45ff; 25:14,19,21,23,30; 26:51. Cf. for *paîs*: Mt 8:6,8,13; 12:18; 14:2.

[15]Cf. Stegemann and Stegemann, *Urchristliche Sozialgeschichte*, 198-204. On the new position of exegesis regarding the popular origins of primitive Christianity, see B. Holmberg, *Historia social del cristianismo primitivo. La sociología y el Nuevo Testamento* (Córdoba, 1995).

[16]Cf. Mt 1:22-23; 2:15,17-18,23; 4:14-16; 8:17; 12:17-21; 13:35; 21:4-5; 27:9-10.

[17]The term *georgós* can mean, more than "laborer" in general, the tenant of a piece of land.

[18]On the theological background that can be hidden behind the idea of appropriation of the fruits, see my commentary on the sin of Adam in *Teología de la praxis evangélica*, pp. 184-199.

[19]Cf. Trilling, *El verdadero Israel*, pp. 75-91.

[20]Cf. the commentary of Juan Mateos in *Nuevo Testamento* (J. Mateos and L. Alonso Schökel) (Madrid, 1987), p. 52.

[21]As is known, a possible etymology of "Hebrew" is *happiru*, a term used in Egypt to designate the inhabitants of the periphery of the empire, who at times were submitted to servitude. For that reason in many texts it preserves a derogatory sociological sense; cf. Gen 41:12; 43:32.

[22]Cf. Mk 6:30-44; Lk 9:10-17; Jn 6:1-14. In the Gospel of Mark, which

serves as a source for Matthew, a second multiplication of the loaves appears (Mk 8:1-10), which reflects the situation of Christianity in Mark's time, when the Judeo-Christian and Gentile communities were still separate. Although Matthew does not know of this separation, he also reproduces the second narration of Mark (Mt 15:32-39), which does not appear in either Luke or John.

[23]Cf. Stegemann and Stegemann, *Urchristliche Sozialgeschichte*, p. 202.

[24]Although Matthew's text is situated in an eschatological context, the distinction between the hundredfold, which is received in return for what has been left behind, and "eternal life" indicates that Matthew probably is still thinking, as Mark most clearly is (Mk 10:29-30), of a transformation which is already taking place in this life.

[25]Cf. Stegemann and Stegemann, *Urchristliche Sozialgeschichte*, pp. 196-204.

[26]See Leif Vaage, "Jesús-economista en el Evangelio de Mateo," *Revista de interpretación bíblica latinoamericana* 27 (1997), pp. 112-129.

[27]Or at least a "paradox," as the commentators are accustomed to say. P. Bonnard, in *Evangelio según San Mateo* (Madrid, 1976), speaks of a "paradoxical bliss" (p. 90).

[28]There has been debate about the "final" character of this judgment, since there is no allusion to the resurrection; the reference therefore may rather be to a judgment which is taking place in the course of history; cf. J. Mateos and F. Camacho, *El Hijo del Hombre. Hacia la plenitud humana* (Córdoba, 1995), p. 151. Nevertheless, the parallels with certain images from Jewish apocalyptic do suggest that it is indeed the final judgment; cf. A. Lasker, "Mateo," in *Comentario bíblico internacional* (Estella, 1999), pp. 1139-1210, especially p. 1201.

[29]Cf. Mt 6:32; 10:5,18; 12:18,21; 20:19,25; 24:7,9,14; 28:19.

[30]Cf. Mt 6:2,5,16; 15:7; 22:18; 23:13-29.

[31]In primitive Christianity, the rich were consistently required to renounce their possessions in order truly to belong to the Christian church; cf. Cyprian, *De opere et eleemosynis*, p. 15.

[32]Cf. Mt 1:2,11; 4:18-21; 10:2,21; 12:46-47; 13:56; 14:3; 17:1; 19:29; 20:24; 22:24-25. We prescind here from the polemic about whether the brothers and sisters of Jesus were in reality some other sort of relatives. In any case, it would be a matter of natural relations of family or neighborhood.

[33]Cf. Mt 5:22-24,47; 7:3-5; 12:48-50; 18:15,21,35; 23:8.

[34]*Elákhistos* is the superlative of *mikrós*, although it comes from an ancient word (*elakhýs*) which also means "little." *Mikróteron* is the comparative, often used in the superlative sense.

[35]Cf. H. B. Sharman, *The Teaching of Jesus about the Future according to the Synoptic Gospels* (Chicago: University of Chicago Press, 1909); T. W. Manson, *The Sayings of Jesus* (London: SCM Press, 1949), pp. 249-251; Ingelaere, "La 'parabole' du jugement dernier," pp. 23-60; G. E. Ladd, *A Theology of the New Testament* (Grand Rapids: Eerdmans, 1974), pp. 118-119; J. R. Michels, "Apostolic Hardship and Righteous Gentiles: A Study of Matthew 25:31-46," *JBL* 84 (1965) 27-37; W. D. Davies, *The Setting of the Sermon on the Mount* (Cambridge: Cambridge University Press, 1964), p. 98.

[36]On the possible broadening of the meaning of the "siblings of Jesus" from disciples to all people in need, see J. Mateos and F. Camacho, *El Evangelio de Mateo. Lectura comentada* (Madrid, 1981), pp. 244-245. Also A. Lasker, "Mateo," pp. 1139-1210, specifically p. 1201.

[37]Cf. Pikaza, *Hermanos de Jesús*, pp. 304-305.

[38]Cf. Antonio González, *Estructuras de la praxis. Ensayo de una filosofía primera* (Madrid, 1997).

[39]Cf. Mt 1:19; 5:45; 9:3; 13:17,43,49; 23:28,29,35.

[40]I am thankful for a suggestion to this effect from Dr. Barbara Andrade.

[41]Cf. J. Driver, *La fe en la periferia de la historia. Una historia del pueblo cristiano desde la perspectiva de los movimientos de restauración y reforma radical* (Guatemala, 1997).

4. The Proclamation of the Reign of Jesus the Messiah

[1]Cf. G. R. Beasley-Murray, *Jesus and the Kingdom of God* (Grand Rapids: Eerdmans, 1986).

[2]Cf. Acts 14:22; 19:8; 20:25; 28:23-31; Rom 14:17; 1 Cor 4:20; Col 4:11; 1 Th 2:12; 2 Th 1:5, etc.

[3]Cf. R. Pesch, *Über das Wunder der Brotvermehrung* (Frankfurt, 1995).

[4]Ancient Zealotry and modern Zionism are also variants of this schema, which at root ignores not only the exhaustion of the state model in the Old Testament, but also the non-violent character of the messianic promises; cf. Is 65:25.

[5]Cf. M. Hengel, *Jesús y la violencia revolucionaria* (Salamanca, 1973).

[6]Cf. Mt 2:2; 21:5; 25:34; 27:11; 27:29-37; Mk 15:12; Lk 18:38; 23:38; Jn 1:49; 12,13,15; 19:14; Acts 17:7; 1 Tim 1:17; 6:15; Rev 15:3; 17:14; 19:16.

[7]On the affirmation of the divinity of Jesus in the New Testament, see Jn 1:1,18; 20:28; Tit 2:13; Heb 1:8-9; 2 Pet 1:1; 1 Jn 5:20. Cf. R. E. Brown,

An Introduction to New Testament Christology (Mahwah: Paulist Press, 1994), pp. 171-195.

[8]In the two quotes from Revelation the majority text says "kings," although modern-day textual criticism prefers "reign"; even so, Rev 5:10 (cf. 2 Tim 2:12) makes it clear that the disciples reign together with Jesus.

[9]The text shows that it is a matter of the justice of God himself (*dikaiosýne autoû*), and not simply the justice of a kingdom separable from God.

[10]See, for example, the position of Martin Buber and of Shalom Ben-Chorim in this regard, in J. Moltmann, *Cristo para nosotros hoy* (Madrid, 1997), pp. 99-100.

6. The Reason for Hope

[1]Cf. Luis de Sebastián, *Neoliberalismo global. Apuntes críticos de economía internacional* (Madrid, 1997), pp. 33-36.

[2]Cf. J. H. Elliott, *Un hogar para los que no tienen patria ni hogar. Estudio crítico social de la Carta primera de Pedro y de su situación y estrategia* (Estella, 1995).

[3]D. Gracia, after analyzing hope in various post-Nietzschean philosophers and theologians, concludes that one of the characteristics of contemporary views of hope is the desire to approach reality in a practical or experiential way. Cf. his article "Pensar la esperanza en el horizonte de la postmodernidad," *Revista de filosofía* 8 (1985), pp. 113-148 and 391-415, particularly p. 407.

[4]It is what Laín calls "the hope of the secularized." Cf. P. Laín Entralgo, *La espera y la esperanza*, 2nd ed. (Madrid, 1958), pp. 188-232.

[5]Cf. E. Menéndez Ureña, *La crítica kantiana de la sociedad y de la religión* (Madrid, 1979), pp. 47, 102. On the motivating character of this idea, see A. Gramsci, *Quaderni del carcere*, vol. 2 (Torino, 1977), p. 1388.

[6]Cf. J. Weiss, *Die Predigt Jesu vom Reiche Gottes* (Göttingen, 1892); re-edited in 1964.

[7]Cf. A. Schweitzer, *Von Reimarus zu Wrede: eine Geschichte der Lebens-Jesu-Forschung* (Tübingen, 1906).

[8]A. von Harnack, *What Is Christianity?* (New York: Harper & Row, 1957), p. 51.

[9]Cf. W. Rauschenbusch, *Christianity and the Social Crisis* (New York: The MacMillan Company, 1997), p. 349.

[10]Cf. W. Rauschenbusch, *Christianizing the Social Order* (New York: The MacMillan Company, 1912), pp. 96-102.

[11]Cf. J. Moltmann, *Das Kommen Gottes. Christliche Eschatologie* (Gütersloh, 1995), pp. 209-217.

[12]Cf. W. Pannenberg, "Erfordert die Einheit der Geschichte ein Subjekt?," in R. Kosellek and W.-D. Stempel, *Geschichte-Ereignis und Erzählung* (Munich, 1973), pp. 478-490, particularly pp. 481-482.

[13]Cf. W. Pannenberg, *Grundfragen systematischer Theologie* (Göttingen, 1967), pp. 86-88.

[14]Cf. Pannenberg, *Grundfragen systematischer Theologie*, pp. 202-222.

[15]Cf. W. Pannenberg, *Anthropologie in theologischer Perspektive* (Göttingen, 1983), pp. 500-501.

[16]Cf. Pannenberg, *Grundfragen systematischer Theologie*, p. 222. On the theology of Pannenberg, see my work "La historia como revelación de Dios según Pannenberg," *Revista latinoamericana de teología* 25 (1992) 59-81.

[17]Cf. J. Moltmann, *Perspektiven der Theologie. Gesammelte Aufsätze* (München-Mainz, 1968), pp. 15-17. Kant had already understood his philosophy of history as an attempt to show that, behind the apparent chaos of history, there was an order willed by God.

[18]Cf. J. Moltmann, *Theologie der Hoffnung. Untersuchungen zur Begründung und zu den Kosenquenzen einer christlicher Eschatologie* (München, 1968).

[19]Cf. E. Bloch, *Das Prinzip Hoffnung*, 2 vols. (Frankfurt, 1959).

[20]Cf. Bloch, *Das Prinzip Hoffnung*, vol. 1, pp. 235-242.

[21]Cf. Bloch, *Das Prinzip Hoffnung*, vol. 1, pp. 237-239.

[22]Cf. Bloch, *Das Prinzip Hoffnung*, vol. 1, pp. 224ff. See also S. Zecchi, *Ernst Bloch: utopía y esperanza en el comunismo* (Barcelona: Península, 1978).

[23]Cf. M. Heidegger, *Sein und Zeit* (Tübingen, 1953), pp. 372-404.

[24]Cf. Xavier Zubiri, *Naturaleza, historia, Dios* (Madrid, 1987), pp. 355-392.

[25]Cf. Moltmann, *Theologie der Hoffnung*, pp. 12-13.

[26]Cf. Moltmann, *Theologie der Hoffnung*, p. 14.

[27]Cf. Moltmann, *Theologie der Hoffnung*, pp. 20-21.

[28]Cf. Moltmann, *Theologie der Hoffnung*, pp. 201-202, 315-319.

[29]Cf. Bloch, *Das Prinzip Hoffnung*, vol. 1, p. 238.

[30]Cf. Moltmann, *Theologie der Hoffnung*, pp. 299-312.

[31]Cf. J. Moltmann, *Der gekreuzigte Gott. Das Kreuz Christi als Grund und Kritik christlicher Theologie* (München, 1987).

[32]Cf. J. Sobrino, *Jesucristo liberador. Lectura histórico-teológica de Jesús de Nazaret* (San Salvador, 1991), pp. 121-232. English translation: *Jesus the Liberator* (Maryknoll, NY: Orbis Books, 1993).

[33]Cf. J. Moltmann, *La iglesia, fuerza del Espíritu* (Salamanca, 1978), pp. 104-106.

[34] Cf. J. Moltmann, *Experiences in Theology. Ways and Forms of Christian Theology* (London: SCM Press, 2000), p. 237; also his "Carta sobre la teología de la liberación," *Selecciones de teología* 15 (1976) 305-311.

[35] Cf. J. Jeremias, *Neutestamentliche Theologie*, vol. 1 (Gütersloh, 1971), p. 101.

[36] Cf. G. R. Beasley-Murray, *Jesus and the Kingdom of God* (Grand Rapids: Eerdmans, 1986).

[37] Cf. H. Merklein, *Jesu Botschaft von der Gottesherrschaft* (Stuttgart, 1983).

[38] Cf. Moltmann, *Theologie der Hoffnung*, p. 201. In the same way, liberation theology points out that the kingdom cannot be gained without the grace of God. Cf. Sobrino, *Jesucristo liberador*, pp. 137-139, 230.

[39] Cf. Moltmann, *Theologie der Hoffnung*, pp. 200-201.

[40] In German, the term "lordship" (*Herrschaft*) suggests a tyrannical state policy, and the root employed (*Herr*) refers only to men, never to women; cf. J. Moltmann, *Cristo para nosotros hoy* (Madrid, 1997), pp. 14, 24. In Spanish the corresponding term, "señorío," can refer both to men and to women (*señores* and *señoras*). We will treat the political problem and theocracy in a subsequent section.

[41] Cf. Moltmann, *La iglesia, fuerza del espíritu*, pp. 232-233; also his book *El camino de Jesucristo. Cristología en dimensiones mesiánicas*, Sígueme (Salamanca:Sigueme, 1993), pp. 144-145.

[42] Cf. Moltmann, *El camino de Jesucristo*, p. 145.

[43] Cf. Moltmann, *Cristo para nosotros hoy*, p. 14. Liberation theology points out occasionally that the most appropriate term to explain the concept in the Old Testament would be that of "reign" (cf. Sobrino, *Jesucristo liberador*, pp. 128-129), but still the concept of "kingdom" continues to be used systematically in the sense of a desired state of affairs, which is already irrupting into history. Cf. ibid., pp. 134ff.

[44] Cf. Moltmann, *La iglesia, fuerza del Espíritu*, p. 233.

[45] Cf. Moltmann, *Das Kommen Gottes*, pp. 202-209.

[46] Cf. Moltmann, *El camino de Jesucristo*, p. 145.

[47] Cf. Moltmann, *Theologie der Hoffnung*, pp. 280-312; *Cristo para nosotros hoy*, pp. 27-28.

[48] Cf. Moltmann, *Theologie der Hoffnung*, pp. 199-200.

[49] Cf. Moltmann, *El camino de Jesucristo*, pp. 371ff.

[50] Cf. J. Sobrino, *La fe en Jesucristo. Ensayo desde las víctimas* (Madrid, 1999), pp. 214-216. English translation: *Christ the Liberator* (Maryknoll, NY: Orbis Books, 2001).

[51] The Messiah now present converts disorganized and despised masses into a structured people, as is shown, for example, in the story of the

feeding of the multitudes (Mk 6:35-44 and parallels). It is not a question of Paul, influenced by Hellenism, forgetting about the masses, as some others would have it (cf. J. M. Castillo, *El reino de Dios. Por la vida y la dignidad de los seres humanos* (Bilbao, 1999), pp. 301ff). It is a question of Paul, as Jewish, knowing that the mission of God for all humanity requires the establishment of a people that provides a real, practical and attractive alternative.

[52]Cf. Antonio González, *Estructuras de la praxis* (Madrid, 1997).

[53]Thus do we reinterpret the "reality" of Zubiri; cf. González, *Estructuras de la praxis*, pp. 23-31, 59-61.

[54]Cf. X. Zubiri, *Inteligencia y razón* (Madrid, 1983). See also the praxeological reinterpretation in my book, *Estructuras de la praxis*, pp. 147-162.

[55]Cf. P. Krugman, *El retorno de la economía de la depresión* (Barcelona, 1999), pp. 171-173. Original edition: *The Return of Depression Economics* (New York: WW Norton and Company, 2000).

[56]Cf. A. Costas, "Más ricos y desiguales," *El País*, January 30, 1999.

[57]Cf. J. L. Segundo, *El hombre de hoy ante Jesús de Nazaret. I: Fe e ideología* (Madrid, 1982), pp. 13-26. English translation: *Faith and Ideologies* (Maryknoll, NY: Orbis Books, 1984).

[58]Cf. G. von Rad, *Teología de Antiguo Testamento*, vol. 2 (Salamanca, 1969), pp. 461ff.

[59]Cf. N. Lohfink, "La ley y la gracia," en *Valores actuales del Antiguo Testamento* (Buenos Aires, 1966), pp. 169-195.

[60]Cf. A. González, *Teología de la praxis evangélica* (Santander, 1999), pp. 127-156, 215-221.

[61]Differently from what happens in the philosophy of G. Marcel; cf. Gracia, "Pensar la esperanza en el horizonte de la posmodernidad," p. 135.

[62]Cf. G. Marcel, *Positions et approches concrètes au mystère ontologique* (París, 1948), p. 49, cited in Gracia, ibid., p. 121.

[63]Cf. J. H. Yoder, *El ministerio de todos. Creciendo hacia la plenitud de Cristo* (Guatemala, 1995).

[64]Cf. Origen, *Commentarium in Evangelium secundum Mattheum*, XIV, 7, in J.-P. Migne (ed.), *Patrologiae cursus completus. Series graeca*, vol. 13 (París, 1857), pp. 1197-1200.

[65]As is well known, "heaven" is a pious circumlocution the Jews use to refer to God. The reign of heaven is the reign of God. Origen understands "heaven" as referring to the higher aspects of the human being (over which God can reign), and not to all of human reality. But he never conceives the reign of heaven as a kingdom in heaven, precisely because

he understands *basileía* as reign, as sovereignty exercised now. Origen was not a Jew, but he knew Greek.

7. The Trinitarian Reign of the Christian God

[1] In theological language, the "immanence" of the Trinity is distinguished from the "economy" of the Trinity. The first refers to the Trinity in itself, independently of its work in the world, while the second refers to its action in the history of salvation.

[2] "Jésus annonçait le royaume, e c'est l'église qui est venue" in Alfred Loisy, *L'Evangile et l'Eglise* (París, 1902), p. 111. In reality, Loisy was criticizing the liberal individualism of Adolf von Harnack, and emphasizing the continuity between the reign of God and the church.

[3] On the interpretation of Genesis 3, see my book *Teología de la praxis evangélica. Ensayo de una teología fundamental* (Santander, 1999), pp. 184ff.

[4] On the socio-political seriousness of this kind of thinking, see P. Krugman, *El retorno de la economía de la depresión* (Barcelona, 2000), pp. 171ff. (Original edition: *The Return of Depression Economics* (New York: WW Norton and Company, 2000.) Also A. Costas, "Más ricos y desiguales," *El País*, January 30, 1999.

[5] As expounded in his *Der gekreuzigte Gott. Das Kreuz Christi als Grund und Kritik christlicher Theologie* (München, 1972), p. 142.